Advance Praise

I used the technique in many f'd up situations to not get arrested, ward off an abusive boyfriend and resolve court cases. They just went away. IT WORKS!
~Anonymous

A few things that struck me immediately are the brevity and that you conveyed quickly and succinctly the method and process. And in the very beginning of the book! It's been my experience with other published modalities that one must read through many chapters of the whys and how comes and the this's, and that's before getting to the crux of the how-to. So I was able to start using the method almost immediately. And even though I was already familiar with the work, your book helped me understand the process in greater depth.

And as you suggested in your writing, this isn't just a heal-it-quick modality. This modality is something that can be employed throughout the day. Whenever I sense a feeling of non-peace, I can do a Remen $\bar{Q}$ process and get settled. And sometimes, when I get to sit in the quiet, I geek out on the process for as much time as I want, playing with whatever comes up unless I'm "working" on something in particular.

Here's the amazing thing; I told my husband about the book and the process and how much I felt it helped me navigate the energies that we've been immersed in. And, bless his heart, he started reading the book and using the process. And this is me testifying that the change in the atmosphere in the house has been dramatic. We are both friendlier, less guarded, more open, and honest. We seem to want what is best for each other.

So from the bottom of my heart, I thank you for sharing this process with me (and the world.)
~Lisa Chandler, Business Owner

This amazing book gives us a tool to easily find inner peace. When we do that, we change the frequency in our space. This heals us on so many levels and miracles often happen. Give yourself the gift of a happier life.
~Lori Aletha, Northwest Psychic Fairs

Great things come in small packages! For over 20 years as a healing professional, I have become familiar with about every healing tool and modality out there to assist one in achieving higher states of consciousness and inner healing. Valeria has brought us full circle with a simple, yet profound tool called Remen $\bar{Q}$, that can easily be utilized by anyone to achieve deep states of inner peace. When in a state of peace, we heal body, mind and *spirit and create coherence between all three aspects. Accessing that innate part of ourselves is nothing less than uncovering our Sacred Selves. It is an immersion of our physicality with the pure Light within. Remen $\bar{Q}$ is an exciting and very effective tool to incorporate into our daily lives. Highly recommend. ~Nathan Z Townley, Spiritual and Wellness Coach. Author of <u>Awakening Within the System - Evolution, Not Revolution</u>*

So many old patterns are emerging for me to be aware of...having this really really helps with relaxing into the heart and not worrying if I can relax and if I can see anything shift.
 ~M. Baker

I must say that I have been using Remen $\bar{Q}$ for a few days now, and I really like the simplicity and elegance. Simplicity however does not dismiss it being very effective. Today I cleared about five patterns from an issue and at the end there was just a smile on my face. I am finding it very helpful. I have studied many so called emotional release ideas and I am to the point that simple is better when it hits the mark. Remen $\bar{Q}$ for me may well hit the mark.
~Jim Adcock, South Sound Wellness

THE REMEN Q̄ METHOD

THE REMEN Q̄ METHOD

An Easy Do-It-Yourself Process to Create Inner Peace and Change Your Reality

Valeria J. Moore

Throughout this book, I have used examples and stories to demonstrate a concept. The names are fictional unless it is about me. These examples represent the patterns I have seen in my work and life experience with others.

ISBN: 978-1-7371275-0-5

Published by Three Moons Publishing
Edited by Barbara Millikan
Interior design by Valeria J. Moore
Cover by Valeria J. Moore

www.remen-q.com

The logo of a heart sitting in the bowl of a crescent represents the timeless nature of the one heart of all sentient beings.

I dedicate this book to all those seeking a joyous heart without boundaries. Without your quest, we would not be asking the next question, taking the next step, bringing ourselves ever closer to a transcendent peace.

Acknowledgments

I want to thank all those who chose to try Remen $\bar{Q}$. Your experiences of peace, calm and joy were part of my journey to understanding Remen $\bar{Q}$.

When humankind is ready for the next step, it manifests in many people's writings. Therefore, I want to acknowledge those writings and practices that focus on alleviating the suffering of the heart.

Barbara Millikan volunteered early in the book writing process to be my editor, waited as I wrote, rewrote the book, and rewrote it again. I am so very grateful for her help. When I was ready to quit, she also provided me with many reasons to write the book about Remen $\bar{Q}$.

My daughter Nikki did a lot of Remen $\bar{Q}$ testing, which provided validation. Her feedback gave me insights into the effects of the Remen $\bar{Q}$ process.

My daughter Denae helped me write "About Me." She has been very supportive in encouraging the completion of this book. In addition, she has reminded me that other books are waiting to be born.

My life partner of 20+ years, Mike, has supported and encouraged my many-pathed journey to inner peace. He has said to me, "I do not understand what you do, but I believe in you." When defeat, fatigue, or illness were part of my journey, that sentence kept me going.

Sue Healy introduced me to Dan Brulé's breathwork. The breathing technique I use with Remen $\overline{Q}$ is from my work with Sue.

My special thanks to the gentleman in Bend, Oregon, who prodded me to use my outside voice to describe, finally, Remen $\overline{Q}$ as a method to transmute a heart of non-peace to peace.

Contents

Question: Why do we need to know the Heart?

Answer: The Heart is the portal to the great mysteries of our being. The Heart plays the song of the DNA. The Heart Sings. The Heart Cries. The Heart hears the heart song of others. The Heart hears the whispers from the soul. The Heart is without end or beginning. The Heart is peace or non-peace. The peaceful Heart is calm and allows the flow of life. The peaceful Heart knows the joy that is within us.

~Valeria J. Moore

Prologue

All of us can work for peace. We can work right where we are, right within ourselves, because the more peace we have within our own lives, the more we can reflect into the outer situation. In fact, I believe that the wish to survive will push us into some kind of uneasy world peace which will then need to be supported by a great inner awakening if it is to endure...So, primarily my subject is peace within ourselves as a step toward peace in our world.[1]

~Mildred Lisette Norman, The Peace Pilgrim

In 1970 I met Mildred Lisette Norman, The Peace Pilgrim. She visited the college I attended at the time. The meeting was in one of my classes. The meeting lasted only an hour, but the Peace Pilgrim has never left me. At 18 years old, I only heard the part of her message referencing the Vietnam War peace effort. Her mission was much greater than that. Her mission was to bring awareness to global peace, living in harmony with the planet, and inner peace. I was more interested in escaping to the next party that day than searching for inner or outer peace.

I have traveled my life journey with The Peace Pilgrim appearing in my memory from time to time. She did not inspire me; she was just there. I was never aware of why her memory was so often with me. I also never asked. My memory of the Peace Pilgrim never seemed to add anything to my life until now. <u>She knew that inner peace was the foundation for global peace and planetary harmony</u>. Her mission lives on in those that seek and find inner peace.

The human tribe has reached a pivotal place on this planet; most people on this planet have neither inner peace nor outer peace. We have been at war with ourselves, each other, and Mother Earth for thousands of years. The planetary resources and climate systems are under assault by human greed. We see a rapid increase in viruses that travel the planet within days. An average of 150 species goes extinct each day[2]. The Earth's temperature has risen 2° F in the last century[3]. Wildfires destroyed 10.1 million acres of forest in 2020 and 4.7 million acres in 2019 in the United States[4]. According to the World Health Organization, 700 million people are at risk of being displaced by drought by 2030[5]. 40% of the world's population is affected by water scarcity[5]. Our external world reflects our inner non-peace.

In the last few years, catastrophic environmental events have seemed relentless in their frequency and magnitude. Yet, it appears nothing is happening to reduce the suffering. We watch the next event that will destroy human life and the environment on an internet-enabled device. We disconnect from the feeling and experience of this destruction. Island and coastal nations around the globe will cease to exist as the seas rise[6]. In 2019 and 2020, there were mass migrations of people from Central America northward due to drought and violence in their home countries[7]. The response by neighboring governments has been to reject these migrants and hurt the people trying to survive. That has happened worldwide to displaced populations.

As a global tribe, we must agree on what's best for the living things on planet Earth, not from a place of 'how do I win' or 'I've got mine.' Recently, I heard an interview on public radio of a woman asking why she had voted for a specific candidate. Her response "My 401K (a retirement account in the United States) is doing great; I don't care about anything else". She was saying, "I win, I've got mine." For humanity to survive, we must come together as one heart with solutions for the health of the soil that grows our food, the air we breathe, the water we drink, and all living things. Only through reaching agreements that serve the planet will we have the possibility of a healthy ecosystem and global peace. When the need is to win, then no one wins, and we all fail. Mildred Lisette Norman, The Peace Pilgrim, believed world peace would come when enough people attain inner peace.[1]

The Peace Pilgrim also believed that extreme suffering would be the catalyst to finally bring us together to create solutions to the worldwide challenges we

now face. Our suffering, our fears can be the catalyst to peace. Only when the global suffering reaches an unbearable level will we, possibly, reach out to find solutions and inner peace. Our survival depends on achieving inner peace and overriding the fear-based responses to environmental and geopolitical challenges. When we come from a place of heart peace, we see the whole. We know that we are all connected. We perceive that what affects the refugee child dying in a leaky raft in the Mediterranean Sea also affects us.

If your heart is at peace, the world will change. Relationships will be compassionate, equanimous, and composed. When you become an emissary of peace, you embrace the wisdom that the water, air, soil and the sentient heart have no country borders. Your relationship with the world changes.

Remen $\bar{\text{Q}}$ is **a tool you can use to create inner and outer peace.** When you are calm and at ease, you can feel the joy that life brings. You are aware of the patterns that stop joy, freedom, and happiness. You can choose to live a life free of chaos and drama by using Remen $\bar{\text{Q}}$. Your inner and outer peace spreads to those around you.

Achieving inner peace is an ancient journey. The ancients knew that peace, inner and outer, is about balance and harmony. Balance and harmony are central to most ancient and indigenous civilizations. When we see ourselves as separate, we lose our peace. We lose our balance and harmony. We lose our sense of connectedness. Each time you attain inner peace with Remen $\bar{Q}$ you take one more step along your journey to an awareness of your nature. You achieve the ability to reflect and 'know' only in a state of peace

Source of the Name
Remen Q̄

The Remen Q̄ Method started as Quantum Neutralization. I wrote a blog article titled 'Don't Heal, Neutralize,'
detailing the process in late 2013. A good friend told me
I needed to change the name and some of the wording. I
had gotten that same message from a group of friends in
Denver; change the name and process wording. Message received.

**I asked myself the question, 'what should I name the
process?'** I heard loud and clear Remen Q̄.' What? I
asked again and heard the same answer. Hmmm, I
thought I'd give it a rest, go back later, and ask again.
After all, the book's content was more important than the
name, and I had a lot of writing before me. I then went
linear; this made no logical sense. What is a remen? I
theorized that the 'Q' meant quantum. I was wrong.
What was the bar over the 'Q'? I headed for Google and
typed in 'remen'. Remen was an ancient Egyptian measurement. What? So began the quest for the understanding of 'remen.'

Remen was not a linear measurement as has been theorized by Egyptologists. The ancients understood that 'remen' was a measurement of our universe's multi-dimensional dynamic nature and its translation across dimensions. Remen was an understanding of the multi-plicity effect of energy as it moved across dimensions. Remen is a conceptual measurement that shifts its quan-tification by the dimensional awareness present. In 9-dimensional awareness, an energetic quantification is different from what would be experienced in 4-dimensional awareness.

'Q' was a nod to our god nature. Q was an 'extra-dimensional' race of beings in the Star Trek TV series and movie. The Q race had many god-like qualities, and among those was the ability to change reality. The Q character, near the end of the series, became a mentor to the humans. A human could join the Q Continuum by evolving and changing their DNA programming if cho-sen by the Q Continuum. This alteration created an as-cension to a higher non-human life form that did not re-quire a physical body.

The bar or vinculum over the 'Q' in mathematical terms is placed over a set of numbers to represent their infinite repetition. In mathematical terminology, it is used to designate the repeating nature of a set of decimal num-bers. In Remen $\overline{Q}$ the vinculum acknowledges the infi-nite nature of awareness.

*Love is what you **think** you feel;*
*peace is what you **know** you feel.*

Introduction

What if the quest to have a pain-free heart is not about love but peace in your heart?

What if peace in your heart changes your reality?

What if the place where you are NOW is the only place to find peace?

What if everything you've learned was noise to keep you from your heart?

You could sum up my entire adult life as a search for peace. In my late teens, I escaped the violent generational alcoholism of my family. Unfortunately, I had not escaped the generational trauma held within me. When the pain, emotional or physical, became intense, I would move on to the next dysfunctional relationship. I knew how to survive relationships of chaos and abuse. I read personal development books, meditated, attended retreats, and did 20+ years of continuous talk therapy. This inner work became another form of escape from my heart pain. These efforts kept me alive, but they did not bring lasting peace.

In 1997 I moved to the Pacific Northwest and found a community open to my consciousness and spirituality explorations. I attended emotional release technique and energy healing courses, taught meditation, traveled to distant lands to learn the foundations of our spirituality, and became a healing arts practitioner and teacher. I read and studied hundreds of metaphysical books on a quest for inner peace and understanding our spiritual nature. Yet, I had a feeling that something was missing no matter how much I read, healed, studied, or meditated. My heart continued to be gnawed by shame, guilt, confusion, humiliation, hopelessness, anger, grief and emptiness.

One morning in the fall of 2013, I awoke knowing that I was no longer a teacher or practitioner of others' healing art methods. I was ill and exhausted. I was not nurturing myself, and my body was failing due to that lack of nurturance.

Shortly before my "retirement," I had set an intention to know a process for an emotional release that was simple and would not create a bypass, a temporary change that led to disappointment. The desired process would also transform all emotional patterns related to an issue at once. Shortly after entering that "wish" into my journal, I heard my inner voice say, 'there's an easier way.' I then experienced a knowing: a series of steps for changing the created patterns of non-peace.

A few days later, I walked a friend through the new process; she experienced an unwinding sensation and light-headedness. She did not like how the release made her feel. I shared the process in a blog article and named the method Quantum Neutralization. I then asked a few people to try it. One person tried it, felt the lightness and a swirling but had no idea what was different. I had no idea what was happening, if anything. So I set the process aside for a few years.

It would not be until 2018 when I realized that this was a method for achieving peace. This process did not dictate a specific outcome. This process was solely focused on the feeling of the heart and being at peace. My view of emotional release therapies required something specific to happen; a stuck trauma response would resolve, or a belief would change to another belief. Unfortunately, I was looking at the process from the wrong perspective. This new process depended on owning the non-peace, setting an intention for peace, and allowing a transmutation to peace.

Remen $\overline{Q}$ starts with you becoming aware that you no longer want to live a life of non-peace. The awareness of non-peace may appear as a life that is full of resistance and is exhausting. Everywhere you turn, there are challenges. You have a life that perpetuates the limiting patterns of your ancestry. Maybe worry is your constant companion. Possibly your health has deterio-rated. Your responses to challenges are reactive and feed the chaos and drama.

The Remen $\bar{Q}$ Method will bring peace to your heart if you own your non-peace, and peace is your intention. You take ownership of the non-peace when you acknowledge that you are the creator of your non-peace. Owning your non-peace does not mean you are respon-sible for the wounding. It means there is a relationship, a connection to the source of the non-peace. There is no fault or blame in this process. You are taking ownership of the relationship. Once you have taken ownership, you have already begun the process of transmuting the non-peace.

When you live with peace in your heart, you open yourself to being present; you open yourself to living in the moment. By being present in the moment, you no longer live a reactive fear-based existence. By living from presence, you change your reality. When you ex-perience heart peace, you extend that feeling to those who may have been the mirror to your fear. You then empower others to move beyond the limitations of fear-based identities. When you live from a place of peace in your heart, creativity and inspiration flow into your life. Your peace becomes my peace.

The Remen $\bar{Q}$ Method offers you 'a way' of living that brings you peace and presence. Your presence in the world will change as you go from reactive to being present. The more present you are, the more you be-come aware of the limiting patterns you created. Once those limiting patterns and associated relationships change to peace, you free up energy for living. The energy trapped in limiting patterns is now free to create and experience joy. Creative and joyful energy becomes the physical change that supports a life of flow.

Your heart is much more than just a muscle. Your heart is an energetic center with a bridge or portal to the soul's universal wisdom, the Akasha. Your heart is the first organ in your body to develop[8]. Your heart, in a state of peace, has an intuitive sense of knowing. Your heart is a center of consciousness that sends and receives information to the thinking-mind and body-mind. Your heart is the sender and receiver of information to other sentient beings. Your heart differentiates between peace or non-peace feelings. Your heart is the seat of the experience of 'kibriya,' divine joy. Kibriya (pronounced kih-bree-yuh) is a knowing of oneness and a feeling of love of all.

I learned of kibriya from Andrew Harvey during a course on Rumi at Wisdom University, now Ubiquity University.

Remen $\bar{Q}$ is not about controlling the future. It is not about manifesting wealth. It is not about controlling others. It is not about forcing a specific outcome. It is not about changing one belief for another. It is not about instantaneous healing of a physical disorder. **Remen $\overline{Q}$ is about inner peace.**

If you want a life of inner peace, Remen $\overline{Q}$ brings you inner peace when non-peace is triggered. **Achieving a life of continuous, uninterrupted peace requires that you commit to the inner work.** First, you must own your reality. You must own that you created your reality. Then use the tools that will bring into your awareness the layers of non-peace created by separation systems: family, institutions, government, corporations, religion, education, etc. Once you know the filters these systems of control have instilled within you, your inner work will move you beyond the filters placed on your perceptions by those systems.

Remen $\overline{Q}$ has been the central part of my consciousness journey for the last four years. I have also woven into my journey meditation, energy healing, drumming journeys, breathwork, Emotional Patterns[13], being in nature, the teachings of many teachers and masters, and occasional bodywork.

Part 1: The 4-Step Process of Remen $\overline{Q}$

The Remen Q̄ Method

The Process

Close your eyes and place your fingertips on your heart space. Then, breathe into presence by taking five slow deep breaths through your nose and out through your nose without pausing using tummy breathing.

1. I am witness to the field of intention to neutralize this created pattern. *(Say this in your inner voice.)*

2. I am witness to the origins of this created pattern *(Say this in your inner voice and visualize a representation of the origin.)*

3. I am witness to the neutralization of this created pattern. *(Say this in your inner voice and visualize a change in the image. Halfway through visualizing the change, __snap__ open your eyes.)*

4. Move your attention to your body and watch until you feel it is complete. *(If there is a sensation of lightheadedness or swirling, allow the sensation to finish.)*

IONS (A Shortcut)

If you have difficulty remembering the process, use the acronym IONS.

> I = Intention
> O = Origin
> N = Neutralization
> S = Snap

After breathing into presence with eyes closed, replace the phrases with the words intention, origin, and neutralization. You may have to do the extended version of the Remen $\overline{Q}$ process a few times, the non-shortcut method, before using the shortcut.

1. **Intention** *(Say this in your inner voice.)*

2. **Origin** *(Say this in your inner voice and visualize a representation of the origin.)*

3. **Neutralization** *(Say this in your inner voice and visualize a change in the image. Halfway through visualizing the change, **_snap_** open your eyes.)*

4. Move your attention to your body and watch until you feel it is complete. *(If there is a sensation of lightheadedness or swirling, allow the sensation to finish.)*

The 4 Steps Expanded

If you feel non-peace or a contraction in your heart and wish to be at peace, *breathe into presence*. Close your eyes. Place the fingertips of your right hand on your heart, bringing your awareness to your heart space. Take five slow even breaths through your nose, keeping your hand on your heart. Use tummy breathing. With each breath, soften or relax the perceived edges of your being. Feel your body's edges blend into the air around you. If you feel unfocused, imagine you can see and feel your breath flow down your body and into the ground under your feet. Then with the out-breath, imagine the air flowing up from the ground and back up your body.

Step 1. Say in your inner voice with your eyes closed: ***I am witness to the field of intention to neutralize this created pattern.*** You are holding an awareness of the contraction in your heart. This contraction is a field of non-peace. The field encompasses everything that is in the intention to neutralize; the created pattern(s). By declaring yourself a witness, you are the observer to the pattern(s) and the intention. This first step in the Remen $\bar{Q}$ process calls in witnessing presence and intention. **The intention is always peace!**

Step 2. Say in your inner voice with your eyes closed: ***I am witness to the origins of this created pattern.*** Visualize the origin causing the contraction; it could be an actual event, a light, a wave, a line(s), a circle(s), a person, a vignette, or a pumpkin. If nothing appears, make something up. Pretend. The imagery of the origin is representative of the created pattern(s). This second step in the Remen $\bar{Q}$ process calls in witnessing presence, intention, and visualization.

Step 3. Say in your inner voice with your eyes closed: *I am witness to the neutralization of this created pattern*. Then create a shift in the visualization. The shift could be to bubbles, a wave of molten wax, sparkles, a colored light, or any other change you create to the visualization. This third step in the Remen $\bar{Q}$ process calls in witnessing presence, intention, transmutation*, and visualization

I have chosen to use the word 'transmutation' to describe the change that happens when your state of non-peace changes to peace. The definition of 'transmutation' is 'to change or alter in form, appearance, or nature and especially to a higher form' per the Merriam-Webster dictionary[9]. The change that happens with Remen $\bar{Q}$ is a higher form of awareness.

Step 4. Approximately halfway through the process of changing the image in your inner vision, **snap** your eyes open. Do this quickly. This process does not lend itself to dawdling in the bubbles, albeit that could be fun. Think 'ninja moves' quick or snapping a rubber band.

Once you have opened your eyes, move your attention into your body. Be aware of any feelings, sensations, shifts, or visuals. For example, you may be aware of swirling or lightheadedness. Keep your awareness of those sensations until they pass.

Important: Once you have done the process above, check-in with your heart. How does your heart feel? Is your heart calm, neutral, or joyous? If so, this session of Remen $\bar{Q}$ is complete. If your heart feels tight, anxious, or contracted, do another Remen $\bar{Q}$ process. The contracted feeling may be very subtle. If the feeling is not calm, peaceful, neutral or joyous, you are not finished. I have found that the number of sessions needed varies.

The experience in your body will vary. You may not experience any sensations after the Remen $\bar{Q}$ process. Or you may feel a significant change.

There is a possibility that you may feel calm and neutral, but you are not necessarily feeling peace. Do a breathing exercise again. Take five deep breaths through the nose without pausing between the inhale and exhale using tummy breathing. This type of breathing is a hybrid of Heart Rate Variable breathing[15]. Then check your heart. Is your heart calm and neutral, or is there a subtle contraction? If there is a contraction of non-peace, then another round of Remen $\overline{Q}$ is needed.

Another part of your body may be the focus of non-peace. For example, pain could be alerting you to a pattern of non-peace when you numb your heart to the non-peace of an unsupportive relationship. For instance, your life partner will not do housework, and the burden falls on you. Subsequently, you may have developed back and shoulder pain. Use your heart or your body discomfort level to gauge your need for more Remen $\overline{Q}$.

Story. I felt frustrated by a loud noise entering my space while I was on the phone for a video medical appointment. Someone in the next room was making a lot of noise, and I could not leave for a quieter space. When I had concluded my discussion, I stood up, and my left ankle had suddenly swollen to twice its size and was very painful. I had never had that happen before. The pain and swelling were so intense I could not walk. I sat back down and did a couple of Remen $\overline{Q}$ processes with my ankle as the focus of non-peace. Within a few minutes, the swelling and pain were gone. The incident had brought up patterns of feeling unsupported and sabotaged while doing something important to me—**the end.**

Why Do I Need to do More Remen Q̄?

The Remen Q̄ process works on the non-peace in your awareness in the present moment. That state of non-peace in your heart or your body may be an experience of many different created patterns. For example, you may feel not good enough, a failure, and shame after a triggering event. Each one of these feelings has a unique pattern. Likewise, these feelings may have many different unique patterns that you identify as one state of non-peace. The Remen Q̄ process transmutes the created pattern(s) that is(are) represented by the visualization. As you transmute the patterns of non-peace, there may be additional layers of created patterns that will now have your attention. The first visualization will probably represent the created patterns of non-peace that have the most intensity.

When you create a limiting pattern, you create the potential for many limiting patterns with the same label. For example, maybe you felt like you could never meet your father's expectations as a child. You felt like you were a failure. That feeling may have started with an ancestor, but you are experiencing the feeling of non-peace. You may have had the experience of failure throughout your life and explicitly failing to meet your father's expectations many times. Each one of these experiences of failing is a unique pattern, a unique vibration. Each time a pattern of failure is experienced, it is a

8

different time, location, type of failure, and maybe, other people. For example, the first time you had the experience of "I am a failure," you were two years old, your father was 30, you lived in Toledo, Ohio, it was in December, and you had dropped a glass of milk. The created pattern "I am a failure" created as a child would have a vibrational pattern that would be different from a pattern created 20 years later in Los Angeles with your boss when you did not deliver a report on time. The two experiences are similar, but they are not the same. So, you will need to run the Remen $\overline{Q}$ process again.

Loss of Focus

If you lose focus while doing a Remen $\overline{Q}$ exercise, you may be holding trauma around trust, identity, change, or deserving peace. For example, you have experienced being blindsided by an old friend. You may feel profoundly troubled by the event. When you try to do a Remen $\overline{Q}$ exercise, you lose focus and can't seem to complete the process. Use the loss of focus as the place of non-peace. Do a Remen $\overline{Q}$ exercise until you feel calm and neutral. Then check the feeling of being blindsided. The feeling of being blindsided may have transmuted to neutral. If not, do the additional Remen $\overline{Q}$ exercise(s) until you feel neutral and calm. The loss of focus may stem from an underlying trauma.

Knowing the Created Pattern

When becoming aware of a created pattern of non-peace and a desire to change that created pattern, you <u>do not need</u> to know the created pattern. Follow your heart or body. Your heart or body will tell you if there is a state of non-peace. Don't overthink the created pattern. For example, suppose that when your mother comes to visit you get a headache. In the Remen $\bar{Q}$ process, you don't need to get to the created pattern to change your heart to peace when your mother visits. Feel the non-peace in your heart or head, and do the Remen $\bar{Q}$ process.

Ancestral Remen Q̄ Process

During a Remen Q̄ session, a DNA strand appeared in my inner vision. As I explored the meaning of that experience, an additional process emerged. The DNA strand, a double helix perceived in your inner vision, is symbolic of a field of information. The field of information is most likely symbolic of an ancestral event that resulted in epigenetic changes. The Remen Q̄ process is then adjusted to reference a field of information.

To use the ancestral Remen Q̄ *process,* breathe into presence using the method given at the beginning of this section.

> **Step 1.** Say in your inner voice with eyes closed: *I am witness to the field of intention to neutralize this field of information* (you continue to hold an awareness of the non-peace you are experiencing).

> **Step 2**. Say in your inner voice with eyes closed: *I am witness to the origins of this created pattern in the field of information*. Then visualize a DNA strand.

> **Step 3.** Say in your inner voice with eyes closed: *I am witness to the neutralization of this created pattern in the field of information*. Then create a shift in the visualization. Change the DNA strand into an

image of your choice (sparkles, bubbles, pink drip-
ping wax, dancing unicorns, a color, etc.).

Step 4. Snap your eyes open halfway through,
changing the imagery. Then focus your awareness
on your body. Watch any sensations as they arise in
your body. Stay focused on the sensations in your
body until they are complete.

How Does Remen $\overline{Q}$ Work?

Imagine standing at the edge of a small creek, and you want to cross to the other side. You step into the creek, and as you step into the creek, your foot breaks the surface of the water. Maybe there is a splash. As your foot comes down on the creek bed, there is a moment, a very brief moment, where the water stopped on one side of your foot. Water will quickly flow into the space created by your foot, redirecting the flow of water. Your foot may have made a swirl of mud, and the pebbles on the creek bed surface have moved. Once you have crossed the creek, the mud finds a new home. Some mud has moved downstream, some has attached itself to your shoes, and some has settled back down to the creek bed.

In the scene above, it appears that nothing has changed; the creek continues to flow. But, the creek changed. It is not the same creek as when you first stepped into the water. Its flow pattern has changed because the pebbles, which defined aspects of the water's movement, and the creek bed mud, have moved. Stepping into a running creek is an analogy for what happens when you do Remen $\overline{Q}$. The water is the relationship that you want to change from non-peace to peace. Just as the nature of water is to flow, it is also the nature of a relationship. A relationship is a flow of feelings that result from created patterns, location (space), and time. When the intention is peace, the most probable possibility for peace is present, waiting to fill the space created by disrupting the relationship's flow. By bringing in the vibration of non-peace with the visualization, you establish the created pattern to be changed. Disrupting the visual representation of the created pattern creates space. Intention moves the vibration of peace into that space. The flow of the relationship is reorganized based on the peace potential that has filled the space. Then by watching your body, you allow the flow of this change to be your new pattern. You are acknowledging the change by witnessing. Just like the creek, there is now a new flow pattern in the relationship.

A relationship of non-peace is like a flooded river. The river is neither calm nor harmonious; it is destructive and dangerous. A non-peace relationship is the same. The created patterns defining a relationship of non-peace are harmful; they take life force. When you use Remen $\overline{Q}$ you are addressing the destructive river of non-peace. You allow peace to flow where there had been non-peace.

And now here is my secret,
a very simple secret:
It is only with the heart
that one can see rightly;
what is essential is invisible to the eye.
~ Antoine de Saint-Exupéry,
The Little Prince

The Fundamentals of
Remen $\overline{Q}$

A Witnessing Presence

*I am witness to the field of intention to neutralize this
created pattern.*

**Presence is a state of witnessing in non-judgment;
witnessing presence.** In Remen $\overline{Q}$, witnessing allows
for a created pattern to be held in expanded awareness
and then changing the observation in that expanded
awareness. Expanded awareness occurs when we are
present. When you are present, your awareness becomes
a deeper understanding of self. While I was writing this
book, I closed my eyes, enabling me to focus on the
moment. I was 'aware' that my fingers seemed like a
field of knowing; there was no longer a definition of
flesh. My heart was centered, calm and relaxed. An
undercurrent of joy filled my being. I felt happy sitting
at my keyboard and birthing a way of peace.

The river of life flows through an open heart.

Story: In 2017, I was experiencing severe knee pain. I had been relying on pain medication to walk and sleep. Then on a visit to my physician, he asked if I was a drug addict. I was shocked. Why did he say that? Why was he saying that? I left that appointment feeling emotionally numb. That feeling of numbness did not leave me. A few days later, I was sitting on the front porch in reflective meditation, and I asked myself, "what is this numbness?" I heard "grief." "Grief? About what?" That second question yielded a flood of information. I witnessed my inner self review the events that had created unresolved grief. I did not argue, get angry, or blame someone or something else. I witnessed grief. In those moments, I understood the power of witnessing and being present to my grief. There was no judgment or analysis of what I could have done better. There was simply a sense of being present to the experience of loss across the spiral of time.

I awoke the following day knowing that the experiences of loss and grief create patterns of repetitive cycles that keep us stuck in aloneness, depression, sadness, anger, denial, and pain. Witnessing presence in this form facilitated my movement through grief – **the end.**

My work with others shifted to witnessing grief. I would sit with a person, create a sensation of expansion in my heart, say nothing and be present to their grief. Witnessing with an open heart created a space where a person's words are sacred and pure without the contamination of judgment or mollification. The words of grief need to be spoken to know that the space filled with pain can be whole again. The spoken words of grief give validation to the invisible wound of loss. In this sacred space, the experience of grief and loss is given form.

In witnessing presence, the energy of stuck grief flows until it dissipates. This transmutation of grief allows the grieving person to transition to the next stage in their relationship.

Story. In the fall of 2017, I met with some friends at a local café. I shared my ideas of witnessing presence with those friends. Suddenly, I felt as if a strong wind had blown open a window. A powerful energy connected one of my friends and me. I listened as one of the friends told me of her loved one's death. In that momentary place, there was only my friend and me. I felt a river of energy flow between our hearts. It was as powerful a connection as I have ever experienced. In that crowded café, there was no one else in the room; there was no other sound, just my friend and me **- the end.**

When you move into the awareness of witnessing presence, what is being witnessed begins to change. This change is an act of creation. The moment you are aware of a created pattern, there is a conscious witnessing of non-peace or peace. In the state of witnessing, you have changed the created pattern. There is a mindful acknowledgment of the created pattern and its effect on you. You choose to continue the created pattern of non-peace or change to a feeling of peace.

How do you achieve a witnessing presence? To be in a witnessing presence, say, "I am witness," still your mind, expand the edges of your being, and be aware of what you feel in your heart. In other words, relax and feel what is in your heart. Use the **'Breathe into Presence'** exercise to still your mind. I have repeated it here, so you don't need to look it up.

Breathe into presence. Close your eyes. Place the fingertips of your right hand on your heart space. Using tummy breathing, take five slow even breaths through your nose without pausing, keeping your hand on your heart. With each breath, soften or relax the perceived edges of your being. Feel your edges blend into the air around you. If you feel ungrounded or unfocused, imagine you can see and feel your breath flow down your body and into the ground. Then with the out-breath, imagine the air flowing up from the ground and back up your body.

Witnessing presence is your soul's desire for union, the union of all your minds (body, heart, and head). It is wholeness. In that space of union and acceptance, the energy of events flows to their resolution without resistance. The information needs nothing else at that moment.

 A story. I am in the checkout line at my local grocery store, and there is a need for a price check. There is no one available to do the price check, and people in the line are becoming impatient and uncomfortable. At that moment, I witnessed, without judgment, the frustration of those in line. Their frustration was my reality. I expanded the edges of my heart while doing the breathing into presence exercise. Anxiety and frustration changed into kindness, calm, and connection for all in that line. I shifted my reality **- the end.**

Another story. I made a recent trip to Portland. When I got to Portland, the traffic had come to a stop. I checked the traffic reports and learned that downed trees from a recent storm were being removed. There was a large truck sitting on my bumper. With each inch I moved forward, the front grill of his truck was all I could see. I could feel his anxiety at being late, and I was anxious because of his grill in my rear window. I owned the situation and changed my reality. I played some lovely relaxing music and remembered a state of bliss from yesterday's Remen $\bar{Q}$ session. In the following moments, as I moved slowly forward, my rearview friend did not move. He created space between our vehicles, and no one moved into that space between us. My new friend followed me that way for the next 20 miles **- the end.**

Witnessing presence is the essence of Remen $\bar{Q}$. When your heart is in a state of presence, it has the potential to transmute reality. The stories above reflect the power of a heart that is at peace. Presence is a dynamic flowing field. When presence meets states born in non-peace, there is entrainment to peace and a sense of oneness.

Witnessing presence is complete awareness of the moment without judgment. In a state of presence, you are not reliving events of the past or projecting the future. You can be neutral to information, where judging that information would set off reactive energy that generates emotions or feelings based on fear. There is only one thing in your awareness, the present and being fully in that moment. You are not judging by pulling in old patterns. You are in a flow of acceptance.

In a state of witnessing presence, you do not need truth. Truth is a judgment. Judgment is separation. Presence is a space of non-judgment, honoring what has priority at that moment. You enter the realm of all possibilities when you enter as a witness with no preconceptions.

Witnessing presence creates a relationship in the universal mind, a relationship defined by a unique vibrational fingerprint. For example, you have a friend who is continuously judging your actions. The judgment from your friend is how they stay safe. Possibly you had a parent(s) that judged your every move. The judgment was your connection to them. If you fell from your bike, you would be called foolish or careless, but that same parent would lovingly clean your knee, apply antiseptic, and then a bandage. Now your friend fills that role of judging your actions. You have a feeling of non-peace in your heart when you hear their judgment. Your parents' created pattern of judgment is different from the created pattern of judgment from your friend. Each experience

21

of being judged creates a new pattern. The vibrational fingerprint, created pattern, of those experiences, may be similar enough to transmute with a single session of Remen $\overline{Q}$. Still, if they are not similar enough, you will need to do additional sessions of Remen $\overline{Q}$ as the pattern of feeling judged is triggered or realized through introspection.

Witnessing presence allows you to access the wisdom in the silence of your being. Presence quiets your being. In the silence, you are allowing yourself to know the wisdom of the peaceful heart. The wisdom of the peaceful heart is a knowing. The knowing may be a whisper of your inner voice. It could be a subtle sensation in your body. It could be a deep sense of peace that you are in the flow of the wisdom needed at that moment.

In witnessing presence, you allow for the possibilities blocked by judgment. Judgment shuts out the possibilities of an alternate awareness. Judgment creates separation by determining a value or quality. A *witnessing presence* is a place of alignment with one's being. Witnessing presence is the place where awareness meets awareness. Witnessing presence does not prevent you from exercising discretion.

Witnessing presence is grace. Grace, the flow in oneness, allows for the infinite possibilities of peace in the moment of witnessing presence. Grace is mindful of what is felt, smelled, seen, heard, or tasted in a moment. Grace does not judge or set a predetermined outcome.

Witnessing presence in Remen $\overline{Q}$ brings you to being witness to your creations. By witnessing, you are affirming the shift in reality. You affirm the change by feeling the peace in your heart.

Neutralization

A friend of mine, Nathan Townley, wrote a book called
Awakening within the System: Evolution, not Revolution. In the chapter "Mastering Yourself," he describes
neutralization.

Page 150
Neutrality is about pausing your emotional-base reactive
cycle long enough to make a choice about your response
and then consciously choose a heart-centered response
versus a linear, fear-based thought and emotion.

Page 151
Neutrality means that we consciously master how we
decide to respond to life and to other people in each
"now" moment.
~Awakening Within the System: Evolution not Revolu-
tion by Nathan Townley[10]

**Neutralization is the process of changing a non-peace
relationship to peace.** A relationship reflects your
peace or non-peace. You have a relationship(s) with
everyone you know and don't know. The Buddha re-
ferred to this as a fishing net, with each person a knot in
the net. A relationship of non-peace is reflecting your
trauma. For example, a friend is in a relationship with a
continually criticizing person. The relationship reflects
limiting patterns of not being good enough.

Neutralization is not a passive process. Neutralization actively makes the conscious choice to own the created pattern causing the contraction in your heart. This process then allows the change to peace. Neutralization happens in the Remen $\overline{Q}$ process by witnessing the transformation of the created pattern(s).

Intention

Lynne McTaggart, in her book *The Intention Experiment: Using Your Thoughts to Change Your Life and the World*, describes intention per the following:

> *Targeting your thoughts—or what scientists ponderously refer to as "intention" and "intentionality"—appeared to produce an energy potent enough to change physical reality. A simple thought seemed to have the power to change our world. (p. xvi)* [11]

> *Every thought we have is a tangible energy with the power to transform. A thought is not only a thing; a thought is a thing that influences other things. (p. xxi)* [11]

Intention is an alert to the universe that you are gathering forces to make something happen. The intention joined with desire creates a flow of meaning. Intention strives to reach a goal that a desire has been set. The intention is the marshaling of energy needed to accomplish the desired goal. For example, I have started making videos to accompany some of my book's topics. Getting the lighting correct for those videos has been time-consuming and has not always worked. So, I set an intention to solve the lighting problem with a minimum investment. Within 48 hours of setting that intention, a quality lighting system came to me. The ease at which I achieved my goal does not mean it fell into my lap. It means I researched various online marketplaces for the appropriate lighting; I made an effort with focused intention starting with a desire.

Intention moves the desired goal to fruition. I have been homebound over the last few months due to Covid 19 restrictions. I have not been to the gym in many months. I would ride my tricycle or take a walk, but my energy was still low, and I was always tired. I 'needed' more energy. So I set the intention of having more energy to accomplish my creative projects. A few days later, a friend called me and told me about an exercise program designed for seniors. I purchased the program, and I showed up to do the daily exercises. My energy level is improving. The results have been better than I expected. The universe got behind me and directed me to the resources I needed to make my intention come to fruition.

Intention starts with a desire, and within that desire is ownership. Before setting an intention for peace, you had a desire to be at peace. You may have stated, "I want this _____ to stop" or "I don't want to feel _____ anymore. " Or you may have realized that you were living a very limiting non-peace pattern such as repeating patterns of sabotage. By using the word 'I,' you have taken ownership of what you are experiencing.

Setting an intention creates a propelling force that energizes the Remen $\overline{Q}$ process. Intention sets in motion the path for changing non-peace to peace. If you make the statement "I intend to..." you imply an action to be committed. In the Remen $\overline{Q}$ process, intent moves from the heart as an active force to change a state from non-peace to peace. Inherent in the Remen $\overline{Q}$ Method is the intention for peace.

An intention for peace creates an alignment to the probabilities that are the frequency of peace. The intention is "the field" of creation. It becomes the place where you can now create your state of peace. Intent narrows the field to just what you perceive at that moment. You are going from non-peace to peace.

Breath focuses the intent. There is a movement of molecules within you in response to the physiology of focus and breath that uses the heart as a place of focus. The snap creates a disturbance, a momentary vacuum. Intention flows into the space left void by the snap to allow the most probable outcome of peace. The change becomes your reality or relationship. Intention allows you to focus the energy of all three minds; body, heart, and thinking. At that moment, by breathing into presence, you bring awareness to all three minds of the peace intention.

Setting the 'field of intention' in Remen $\overline{Q}$ allows intention's intelligence to align with potential possibilities for peace. There are multitudes of possibilities for non-peace and peace within the relationship field. The field of intention aligned to peace filters those potential possibilities to the most probable transmutation of the relationship to peace. For example, a friend of mine has a co-worker that is continually criticizing her. The criticism causes her to question her work and feel not good enough. As a result, she hates going to work and wants to quit. My friend owns the relationship and uses Remen $\bar{Q}$ to transmute the non-peace to peace. The next day when she goes to work, she finds out that the co-worker has transferred to another division of the company in another state. This resolution is only one of a myriad of possibilities for peace. For example, the work situation stayed the same, but my friend no longer felt non-peace when the co-worker was critical. Or the co-worker no longer felt the need to be critical.

In the universe, there is an immeasurable, indescribable force which shamans call intent, and everything that exists in the entire cosmos is attached to intent by a connecting link.
~Carlos Casteneda

Visualizing the Created Pattern

Visualization is the inner process by which you observe a created pattern's vibratory representation and then witness the shift of that vibrational definition in your mind's eye. When you visualize the created pattern in Remen $\overline{Q}$ you bring intent, focus, awareness, acknowledgment, and knowing to the impending transmutation.

I am witness to the origins of this created pattern.

Visualization brings awareness to the non-peace. Awareness is the perception of a relationship that has previously been unacknowledged. The relationship with non-peace has been there, but now awareness says, "This is non-peace. I own this. I am ready to create a new reality of peace." Visualization focuses awareness on the created pattern(s) that is(are) non-peace. What you observe is the reality you have created.

When I began writing emotional states for <u>Healer Wisdom</u>, I would see an image symbolic of an emotional state. These images were often complicated vignettes that held the vibrational pattern for a disease's created patterns and emotional states. I would record the image details and then analyze the symbolism. I would then synthesize the information derived from the symbols into an emotional state. When you engage in Remen $\overline{Q}$, you have decided to own the pattern causing the non-peace. You may not know the source of the pattern, but you acknowledged that you created this reality. Even if it is dancing unicorns with rainbows, the origin's imagery brings the vibration of the created pattern into your inner awareness and intent. The image in your mind's eye is the vibrational match to the created pattern present in the heart experience of non-peace.

All created patterns have an origin. The origin could be trauma from the current life or ancestral and carried forward through the familial belief systems or reside epigenetically in your cells. The picture that you perceive in your mind's eye represents the origin of the created pattern. That image may be a memory, or it could be symbolic of the created pattern. When you visualize the origin of the created pattern, you bring the power of presence to the created pattern of non-peace.

Transmutation of the Origin

Once you have witnessed the origin representation, you use your imagination to change the origin imagery. The origin is in a state of becoming. Then when you snap open your eyes, you create a vacuum. This vacuum is the space between when something happens and something begins. This gap is the deep sweet silence where there is no thought, where the formless becomes form.

I am witness to the neutralization of this created pattern.

When you bring awareness to a pattern that is non-peace, it begins to change. In Remen $\overline{Q}$ you change the image representing the origin of the created pattern causing a state of non-peace. You are shifting awareness from one state to another, powered by the intention of peace.

The visual that you perceive represents the origin of the non-peace, and the act of visualizing starts shifting the non-peace to peace. By visualizing and setting the intention to neutralize the created pattern, you have acknowledged a pattern of non-peace. That acknowledgment has shifted the awareness of the pattern. That shift in awareness has started the transmutation to peace.

Out beyond ideas of wrongdoing and right-doing,

there is a field.

I'll meet you there.

When the soul lies down in that grass, the world is

too full to talk about.*

~Rumi

*The Rumi quote above is a snippet from the poem

"A Great Wagon."

Awareness of the Body

Be aware of how your body feels

After snapping open your eyes, you move your awareness into your body to complete the Remen $\bar{Q}$ process. When you observe the change from non-peace to peace, you bring peace into your reality.

When you shift your awareness from the changing created pattern imagery, you are fully present to the sensations in your body. You may experience a feeling of lightness or lightheadedness as your physical self adjusts to the new sensations of peace and the neutralization of the created pattern. Some have described a spiral sensation or an unwinding.

When you snap open your eyes, you are disconnecting from the created pattern of non-peace. At the snap, you are getting out of your way. When you let go of the created pattern, the 'field' becomes the intention of peace. At that moment, the most probable possibility becomes the peace you intend.

When you focus your awareness on the body sensations, you are completing the shift to peace. That shift is the awareness that the initial state of non-peace is now reflecting a new possibility of peace.

34

After the sensations in your body have finished, you then move your awareness to your heart. You will then be aware of the feeling of peace or non-peace held there. If you are still experiencing a contraction in your heart or any new non-peace physical sensation, you will want to do another Remen $\bar{Q}$ process. Your heart or your body tells you if you are now at peace or non-peace. For example, after completing a Remen $\bar{Q}$ process, you feel tension at the base of your skull. Use the information from the body to inform your progress.

You are allowing the creation of peace.

After years of working with the Remen $\bar{Q}$ Method, I do not experience the lightness or unwinding as frequently as when I first started. Anecdotally, I have heard this from others also. Therefore, your experience with the flowing of energy may vary.

Be the peace you wish to see in the world.
~Martin Luther King, Jr.

Helpful Hints

Don't Overthink

Don't overthink the visualization. Overthinking creates doubt. Doubt will sabotage the process. If no visual appears, then pretend you see something. Use the first thing that comes into your mind's eye. The first image is a symbolic representation of the created pattern.

When you have finished a Remen Q̄ process, and you notice that your heart is still constricted, there are more non-peace created patterns being held. These created patterns could be additional layers of the origin, or they could be additionally created patterns that have been in the background of created patterns that were more intense. Continue the Remen Q̄ process until you feel peace in your heart.

You Do Not Create a Specific Outcome

The outcome of a Remen $\bar{Q}$ process is based on the intention of peace and the most probable possibilities for peace at that moment. This process is not about replacing one pattern for another. For example, you get a headache when visiting your mother because her judgment triggers a feeling of not being good enough. You may have created patterns of 'I'm not good enough for my mother.'; 'Everything I do is wrong.'; 'My mother always judges me.'; etc. The list of created patterns could be quite long. Remen $\bar{Q}$ does not take the created pattern of 'I'm **not** good enough for my mother' and replace it with 'I **am** good enough for my mother.' With Remen $\bar{Q}$ you are declaring an intention for peace. The outcome is peace. The pattern of 'I'm **not** good enough for my mother' has transmuted to peace.

Part 2: The Way of Remen $\overline{\text{Q}}$

A Way

The Remen Q̄ Method offers you a 'way' of living that brings you peace and presence. Your heart, when living Remen Q̄ as 'a way,' becomes your guide, your peace messenger. When your heart is calm and neutral, you are at peace. When your heart is contracted, you are feeling fear. The reality you are experiencing at that moment is fear. For example, you are worried, and your heart feels anxious or contracted. Worry may be a created pattern that you experience often.   By using Remen Q̄ at the moment of contraction, you change your experience of reality to peace.

We achieve heart peace by reconnecting to nature, breathing, journaling, working with the Akasha, meditation, ancient forms of movement, Remen Q̄, and wisdom teachings. Wisdom teachings may embrace the use of sound, energy medicine, movement, or shamanistic practices* to unblock the connection to our heart-soul wisdom. These practices allow us to see the aspects of self that create obstacles to our heart peace. They also allow those obstacles to transmute.   These practices quiet our being. When we achieve quiet, we can hear our inner voice tell us what keeps us from heart peace at that moment when we ask. We then have the opportunity to change the states of non-peace using inner technologies.

There are many more practices from the ancient wisdom teachings not mentioned here.

When I awake in the morning, I go to my meditation space. I meditate, journal, and read. During my morning time, I check in with my heart. Is there contraction or expansion? Did my readings, dreams, journal writing, or meditation trigger anything that I need to address? I observe my heart, and if non-peace arises, I will spend the few seconds needed to change my awareness to peace. As a "practice," I have found that if non-peace arises, it must be addressed. I am no longer numb to the sensation of a contracted heart. A contracted heart is very uncomfortable and gets my attention. The Remen $\bar{Q}$ Method has become a 'way' for me. I call this my peace hygiene.

Sometimes the sensations of non-peace are subtle, almost imperceptible. The practice of Remen $\bar{Q}$ creates an awareness of slight heart contractions that in the past would have been ignored. Using Remen $\bar{Q}$ to transmute these subtle contractions of the heart will yield changes in your inner peace. You do not need to know the source of the contraction. You only need to set the intention for peace, own the non-peace, and do a Remen $\bar{Q}$ exercise until there is peace.

Story: I went to the grocery store to pick up a few items for dinner. I selected my food items and went to the checkout line. I was the fourth person in line waiting for checkout. I disappeared into my inner world, disconnected, and did not notice what was transpiring around me. The pain in my knees brought me back to an awareness of the delays happening at the head of the checkout line. My first awareness was irritation and a growing frustration held by the other people in line. A caretaker was training people in her care how to pay for groceries. I could feel the energy of frustration building. People's faces were tight and unhappy. At that moment, I took responsibility for what I was sensing in my heart. I briefly closed my eyes and did a Remen $\bar{Q}$ process on the contraction in my heart. In the next few seconds, the energy shifted. People put down their phones and began to talk to one another. I saw smiles and heard laughter. One person recited a funny story. Then, the people in that line started helping each other—**the end.**

Reflection: The tension felt by the people in line was a reflection of my reality. I had created a reality of tension and frustration. I shifted my non-peace to peace with Remen $\bar{Q}$ and brought an awareness of oneness and connection into my heart. When I owned the reality, I created a 'way' of peace. I had no expectations of the outcome.

When living from the heart and using Remen $\bar{Q}$ as a 'way,' you practice a mastery of self. You become the master of your feelings. Your feelings no longer create a reactive mind. Instead, life becomes joyful and flows. A life that flows is not stopped by obstacles but flows around obstacles or transmutes to flow. Challenges become events of synchronicity.

41

You consciously live your life purpose. You may find yourself with a feeling of the grace of purpose, a purpose that feels inspired. You align your thoughts, feelings, and emotions to your purpose of being. There's a feeling of coherence in your thoughts, feelings, and emotions.

Your heart softens to kindness for all. Changing your relationships of non-peace allows joy. You witness your actions with clarity. You will see others in a whole new way. Within those experiences of witnessing others, you will know yourself and what keeps you from peace. In a state of peace, you observe and then do what is necessary. You are more aware of the inner nature of others around you.

You no longer hide your eyes from others in some act of ancient ancestral fear. Instead, you connect in those spaces that acknowledge another's humanity. When you connect to others with your eyes, you connect to their heart.

Decisions are no longer reactive responses. Instead, decisions are made from the conscious awareness of peace.

When you enter the space of presence in the Remen $\bar{Q}$ process, you are in a state of peace that opens you to the infinite possibilities of peace. You are the peace you wish to become. You do not drive or determine the specific possibilities. Instead, there is a flow of energy that creates and supports life. There is an intelligence within the intention to move from non-peace to peace.

If you choose, Remen Q̄ can become a journey to a heart free from fear when lived as a 'way.' Your life's journey is guided by the heart to free your heart from non-peace. The non-peace in your heart is trauma, attachment, etc. When you experience non-peace, you experience it as a contraction in your heart. Your heart-mind will send a message of the contracted feeling to your thinking-mind and the body-mind. Your thinking-mind will place a label of anger, depression, worry, sadness, betrayal, etcetera on the message from the heart-mind. Your body-mind will then respond to the identified feeling. For example, you experience a heart contraction. Your thinking-mind recognizes this sensation as a feeling of betrayal. Your body-mind reacts with stomach pain and a contraction of your belly. At this point of awareness, you now choose to continue in non-peace or take back your peace. If you decide to take back your peace, you have set the intention for peace. When you witness the origin of the non-peace feeling, you focus the power of intention on the pattern creating limitations. For example, in your visualization, worry might look like an ancestor wringing her hands over an unexpected bill or sitting at the bedside of a very sick child. Worry and the intention to change the worry to peace brought you to this image. This image is the vibrational representation of the created pattern of worry. During the visualization, you change the pattern by watching the image partially shift. The power of intention for peace takes

43

over when you rapidly release the modified image in your inner vision. At that moment, you disrupt the pattern and allow intention to flow peace.

Story: Gina is a "giver." Gina gives and gives to the point of exhaustion. She feels like she gets nothing back in return. She feels alone, resentful, unloved, and rejected when she thinks that her giving has not gotten her what she wants in the way she wants it. Over time Gina develops debilitating fatigue due to the out-of-balance giving. Being the "giver" was a role she created in her childhood family. The "giver" identity is non-peace. In this role, she had adopted a victim identity; everyone else was to blame for how she felt. Gina knew this about herself, but she repeated the same pattern after working for years to change.

When she was finally ready to let go of being a 'giver' and victim, she set the intention for peace by engaging the Remen $\bar{Q}$ Method. During the visualization, she saw a vignette in her past where being a 'giver' was how she escaped the wrath of an emotionally impaired parent. Her relationships, once based on a 'giver and taker,' are now different. One of those relationships was with a co-worker that took advantage of Gina's giving nature. That relationship changed to one of respect and considerateness—**the end.**

What's the Purpose and Effect of Remen Q̄?

The purpose of Remen Q̄ is to bring you to a heart that feels peace and allows for the infinite possibilities of peace. When you engage the Remen Q̄ Method to address a feeling of non-peace, you are not declaring an outcome. You are setting an intention of peace. For example, you have a pattern of worrying every time your teenage son gets behind the wheel of the car. If you engage in a Remen Q̄ process to shift your worry, you are not setting an outcome that your son will never get into an accident. Instead, you are setting an intention that your heart is at peace when he gets behind the wheel of a car. Changing your state of non-peace to a state of peace may result in any one of potentially hundreds of different outcomes. The most probable outcome is that your heart is calm and neutral. You no longer perceive your reality with an anxious heart. When you are calm and peaceful, you are removing the charged and reactive energy of non-peace. You are changing your reality and the physical manifestation of your non-peace to a peaceful calm.

For example, your landlord sends you a notice that the rent will increase by 10% starting at the end of your current lease in two months. Your budget cannot take a 10% increase in rent. You become very stressed and angry. You become reactive and immediately begin thinking about having to move. You lose your peace and start yelling at the landlord. The landlord reacts with anger at your yelling, and a week later, you receive a 60-day eviction notice.

Alternative: Instead of becoming angry after receiving the rent increase notice, you sit for a moment and do a Remen $\bar{Q}$ process until you feel neutral in your heart. You then decide to talk to the landlord and determine if there are options to keep the rent the same amount. The landlord explains that he has just received notice that there will be a significant increase in the property taxes, and the apartment building needs some expensive maintenance. These bills will wipe out all of his profit for the coming year. Your landlord is retired and depends on the apartment building's income to support him and his wife. As you talk, the landlord offers you another option. He has another apartment that will be available very soon that is smaller, but the rent will be the same as what you are currently paying. That apartment is a desirable unit for you as it is on the ground floor, and your knees are beginning to get painful. You would not have to come up with the first and last month's rent plus the security deposit if you were to move. The situation has resolved to only one of many possibilities for peace.

Remen $\bar{Q}$ becomes 'a way' of being in the world. Remen $\bar{Q}$ becomes a daily practice if you are committed to alleviating your heart's suffering. Remen $\bar{Q}$ is a way out of suffering. Remen $\bar{Q}$ invites you to bring peace to that part of you that mirrors the suffering of others. When you create peace within, you change your relationship to suffering. You bring peace to relationships that are suffering. While your contribution may seem small, there is a butterfly effect with any change in the heart. The butterfly effect is where a small change[12] can have significant effects elsewhere. What may seem like a tiny change of shifting a relationship from non-peace to peace may change another person to feeling peace. That shift could then turn the non-peace state of multiple relationships into peace.

It isn't enough to talk about peace. One must believe in it. And it isn't enough to believe in it. One must work at it.
~Eleanor Roosevelt

What Will Remen Q̄ Do for You?

Empowerment

Remen Q̄ empowers you to reclaim your inner peace.
If you choose to do so, you can shift the feeling of
'helpless or hopeless' to 'I am in control of my peace.'
When you feel empowered, you do not feel defeated in
the face of challenges. When you are empowered, you
are in alignment with values not based on fear. When
you are empowered, you have a sense of self-
determination, you feel free to act without outside influence. Empowerment means you have an awareness of
options or choices. Choices are then made in alignment
with a heart at peace. When you feel empowered, you
can sit in harmony with others and align with what is
needed at that moment without resistance. There isn't a
feeling of "I must win."

**Empowerment may not be 'doing'; it may be 'not do-
ing.'** In this case, by not engaging, you are 'not doing,'
and yet it is an active choice. Being at peace during a
storm of emotions brings the possibility of peace and
compassion to the relationship.

Empowerment brings you to an understanding of oneness. Oneness is a worldview that we are all one. We are all connected. There is no 'real' separation between you and a person on the opposite side of the world. Within oneness, empowerment is mirrored back to you in relationships with others that also feel empowered. When you bring empowerment to a relationship, you bring peace.

Empowerment opens your awareness to understanding. When your heart is at peace, you allow, without resistance, different possibilities. You have choices. Your responses are not reactive. This presence is a conscious presence, not anchored in a contracted heart.

Empowerment is not power. Empowerment is knowing, confidence, and peace. Empowerment comes from within. Empowerment is undaunted by those that would strive to perpetuate systems of power. Power is based on fear and a need to be safe by being in control. Power is from external sources such as religious, government, ancestral, cultural, or corporation institutions. These institutions bestow power based on a paradigm of fear. Power will degrade, and control will disintegrate. Relationships based on power are based on fear. For example, religious and social institutions have seen their influence degrade in recent years as their leaders' decades of child sexual abuse have been made public. Ancestral power degrades when a scion of the family dies or becomes impaired. Corporate power degrades when a corporate leader breaks the law.

Our sense of empowerment is systematically destroyed by schools, cultures, religions, families, and governments when judgment and a lack of trust are instilled. Based on control, institutions judge people by gender, career, education, religion, economic status, race, body type or age.   Judgment implies separation and a false hierarchy. Thus, judgment is a tool of disempowerment when you feel judged and when you judge. When you feel judged, you feel rejected and isolated. When you judge, you confine yourself to a limited identity and perpetuate the institutional systems that disempower you.

When a society or government treats people differently because of their race or gender identity, this treatment becomes a discrimination system that disempowers people. That same system that disempowers others stops energy flow for the people and institutions doing the discrimination.   These institutionalized systems then create a devitalized system that will eventually degrade and self-destruct.   Worldwide disempowerment systems have started to implode as the population demographics shift away from a dominant male Caucasian culture.

In my work with clients and creating <u>Emotional Patterns</u>[13], the engrained powerlessness pattern and feeling disempowered are elements in many disorders. 'Disempowered' is a feeling of no choice.   Powerlessness is a feeling of no control. The feeling of being disempowered and powerless has a great deal of power to create dysfunction and disease. For example, feeling powerless and disempowered can be a mask for anger. You may have learned, as a child, that expressing anger resulted in punishment. You learned that to be safe, you had to hide your anger. Hiding anger becomes associated with a pattern of feeling as if you have no choices and are disempowered. The energy of hidden anger gets held in the body and a person's interaction in relationships.

Anger creates an inflammation that can be associated with diseases in every system in the human body. For example, the very first malady in the <u>Emotional Patterns</u>[13] book gives an emotional state for an abdominal aortic aneurysm (p. 27), which reflects feeling anger and powerlessness:

> *False hopes about their life become too much to bear as their life wanes. They commit inner suicide as the hurt and anger explode on the inside. What should have been joy becomes nothing but pain, anger, and hatred in the face of being powerless. The pain of living becomes too much. Held out to others as unworthy. Feels subjugated, humiliated, and is possibly physically abused.* [13]

Unresolved anger associated with feeling powerless creates destructive relationships. Instead of addressing the anger, the anger is hidden. Hiding or suppressing anger is a reactive pattern that does not allow for resolving the anger. Relationships will perpetuate the experience and pattern of feeling angry, disempowered, and powerless. For example, a person is served undercooked cold food when the food should be hot. The waitress is rude and refuses to do anything to fix the problem. The person becomes angry but keeps it to themselves. They do not feel like they have any control or choices in the situation. So they pay the bill and leave without contacting the manager to fix the low quality of the food. This person will keep attracting these types of experiences with relationships and restaurants.

Shifting Reality from Non-Peace to Peace

When your heart is contracted, your reality is based on fear. The fear causing your heart contraction may be based on an immediate instinctual survival response. If that is the case, then that fear response may save your life. However, suppose the fear-based heart contraction is not an immediate survival response; you are re-experiencing an earlier life trauma. It could also be an ancestral or epigenetic influence. The lens through which you perceive and create your reality is colored with the fear held by memory. You or your ancestor survived the trauma that is now affecting your perceptions. For example, my grandmother saved everything. She kept coffee tins, margarine tubs, string from the top of flour bags, and the flour bags' fabric. She had drawers of bread wrappers and twist ties. My grandmother threw very little in the trash. I can still hear her say, "You never know when you will need that." She had lived through a time in history, The Great Depression of 1929 to 1939, when there was no food, no fabric for clothing, there was nothing. It was a time of great angst, social upheaval, and the trauma of lack and loss. For me, this became an inherited fear around food scarcity. I would gather food like a squirrel preparing for the winter. I would carry energy bars in my purse. Before a one-hour hike, the backpack I prepared contained fruit, chocolate, nuts, energy bars, and sandwiches. My kitchen shelves were filled with food, and my car would always have food stored in both side doors and the front pocket. My sweetie had confronted me on many occasions about the overstocking of food, and I would respond, "You never know when you will need that." I feared not having enough food to eat. I inherited the fear of starvation from my ancestors. As I live through a time of insecurity in the world, I am at peace, and I have what is prudent to take care of my family. I no longer have stashes of food in the car, my home office, or my purse.

When you feel at peace, you are more aware. You are more connected to the world around you. You are no longer unconsciously reacting. You become more in tune with the messages from your heart. When you are at peace, you open yourself to a whole new level of sensory information. Your 'way' in the world becomes more mindful and observant. When an action or a response is needed, it comes from a peaceful heart. You no longer give energy to the trauma-dramas. Your awareness is not coming through a filter of fear.

You are the observer and the creator of your reality.

Remen $\bar{Q}$ creates an active sense that you are creating your reality. Your view of reality and the intensity of feeling you apply to your life events is influenced by your memories, traumas, and ancestral influences. Patterns of limitation are based on those influences. For example, as a child, you may have had the experience of growing up with an alcoholic parent. You developed survival strategies that kept you safe within the repeated chaos, anxiety, and possibly violence. These survival strategies have created patterns of non-peace in your adult life. As a child, you experienced turmoil and violence during the night due to an alcoholic parent. As an adult, you have insomnia and often anxiety during the night. Remen $\bar{Q}$ applied to the limiting patterns of chaos and emotional pain can take your life experience from non-peace to peace.

Story: I have family members who live in the Bay Area of California, and I visit as often as possible. The stress level in this area of the world has been unbearable for me for many years. I would often opt to drive to the Bay Area from Washington State, over 800 miles, to not have to get on an airplane and leave as soon as my anxiety became overwhelming. It was easier for me to drive 14 to 15 hours than to get on a plane. Being on an airplane for a 2-hour trip created more stress than a 14-hour drive. After a few hours into a visit, I would feel emotionally shut down and have a tough time enjoying my family. My nerves would feel raw, and I wanted to run away from the intensity. As a child, I found ways of 'running away' when the stress became overwhelming.

A trip to California in 2018 reflected the changes I have made in my reality. My ability to drive a long distance had become impaired due to physical issues. So to see my family, I had to take an airplane. The airplane trip was a breeze, and I was not emotionally overwhelmed. I felt like I had the most fun I have had connecting with my grandchildren a long time. I was unfazed by the intensity of California. In one incident during my visit, I was sitting in the car waiting for my daughter while she picked up a to-go order of food. A car pulled up beside ours and parked. The passenger had trouble getting out of the car. The driver had parked too close to my daughter's car. The driver lost his peace. He stood in front of the car and started yelling at me as I sat in the passenger seat, calling me names and making threatening hand motions. I felt calm, neutral and curious. I stayed in a place of quiet calm without engaging in his crazy. I was present but not feeding or engaging the crazy. He walked away after a few moments—**the end.**

What Are You Shifting?

When you shift your reality using Remen Q̄ you move from a place of non-peace to peace. Peace is neither fear nor love. Instead, peace feels neutral and calm. Peace is an ease that flows instead of resisting.

If you are at peace with yourself,
You will discern peace around you.
~Sri Sathya Sai Baba

When you change a state of non-peace to peace, the non-peace *relationship* will change to peace. By changing your non-peace in your relationship to others with Remen Q̄ you remove your part in the chaos, fear and toxicity. Your reality changes because the relationship changes. Your relationships reflect your state of either peace or non-peace. When a relationship becomes one of peace, then peace is felt by the person making the change. You have removed your fear from the relationship. Changing your feelings to peace does not mean that the other person will feel peace. They may have created an identity around the state of non-peace. For example, a parent has an adult child that depends on them to bail them out of financial trouble. This pattern is creating a drain on the parent's bank account and stress in their relationships. The parent decides to own the co-dependency and the stress it is creating. The parent applies the Remen Q̄ Method until they feel a calm take over their heart. They no longer feel the need to give

57

money to the child. Changing the created pattern of non-peace to peace will allow a new range of possibilities to unfold where the parent is no longer providing money to their adult child.   The parent no longer plays with the adult child on the drama and fear playground when their child has created financial chaos.   The parent is no longer part of a codependent relationship.

Story: Mike, my life partner, and I live in an Oregon suburb, and the house behind us is a rental. There has never been an issue until late 2016 when a new group of people moved into the house. Their driveway was within a few feet of our bedroom window. The 'father' brought with him many people; we never knew how many people lived there. The 'father' brought a logging truck, which was illegal, and approximately six cars blocked the sidewalks. The logging truck would start between 1 a.m. and 3 a.m., run for at least 15 minutes before leaving, at least five days a week outside my bedroom window.   The sound would cause our whole house to vibrate, and if a window were open, it would fill our home with diesel fumes. I would get a strange sensation inside my head as if someone had a toilet plunger placed over each ear and the toilet plungers were being pumped when the logging truck engine was started. I was getting abysmal sleep, and my blood pressure was becoming dangerously high.

I started calling and emailing city code compliance to have the logging truck moved. I called and emailed the city compliance officials many times. The police and code compliance showed up several times. Nothing changed.

Then in early 2018, I made the conscious decision that I created this situation. I created this pattern. I could not fathom what pattern I held to attract this situation, but I would own it anyway. I did the Remen $\bar{Q}$ process. In a couple of days, the truck disappeared, and so did the people living there. The new neighbors were quiet, and my nights became peaceful. I was able to stop the blood pressure medicine, and my blood pressure returned to normal—**the end**.

When you remove your patterns of non-peace in a relationship, you allow for the possibilities of peace. You move to a place of trusting yourself, and in that peace, there is no projection of what might happen. There is trust in the process of allowing peace. The story above demonstrates that I shifted the reality of something happening to me and me playing the victim to being the creator of my reality. My angst at the open hostility and disregard for others held by the neighbor fed the chaos. When we engage in turmoil and fear, we become entangled with those created patterns. I did not consciously intend for the solution that happened. This outcome was only one of many possibilities that could have happened that would have created peace.

Inner Peace Becomes Outer Peace

Outer peace is created by changing the patterns that reflect inner non-peace. There are two states of being; peace and non-peace. Non-peace is contracted, disharmonious, dualistic, and disconnected. Peace is a state of balance, flow, and oneness. When you respond from a state of non-peace, your decisions and actions are reactive. Reactive responses create non-peace. When you respond from inner peace, you open yourself to conscious awareness found in the inner silence of your heart, body, and mind. When you feel inner peace, you are more aware of your feelings. You are no longer unconsciously reacting. You become more in tune with the information from your heart. Peace allows emotional clarity in your thoughts and feelings. When you are at peace, you then open yourself to a whole new level of sensory information. Your 'way' in the world becomes active, observing, and mindful. When an action or a response is needed, it comes from your heart. You no longer engage in trauma-dramas. When you transmute a state of non-peace to peace with Remen $\bar{Q}$ you change your reality of a chaotic relationship to a probability of peace. Reality changes because your relationship changed.

Purpose

Our purpose is to create connections of peace in a state of presence. In February 2020, I attended one of the gem and mineral shows in Tucson, Arizona. I stopped in one booth, and behind me, I became aware of one of the shop owners telling another shop owner of an incident that had just happened. An attendee had walked up to her and screamed at her that she should go back to China. There was no hesitation, no thought, no conscious choice. I walked up to her and told her I had overheard her conversation. I began sharing that I had a homemade version of an essential oil blend purported to be anti-viral and could be helpful, seeing as she would encounter hundreds of people during the gem show. I shared the essential oil blend with everyone there. The next thing I knew, I had a small crowd of women, and I taught them how to make this blend. One woman in the group recognized the blend as a version of Thieves Oil. There were smiles, warmth, presence, and a heartfelt connection of peace.

Once you shift to a 'way' of peace, there is purpose. Purpose is a steady energy flow applied to a specific focus and direction. When your heart is at peace, you live your life with purpose. You have a knowing of what needs to be done. The path of peace is one of knowing, where actions are conscious and deliberate. There is clarity of vision, and your intention is always peace. You are not motivated by fear in your efforts.

Your purpose is not a specific occupation but a call from the heart. For example, a friend of mine was a teacher in a very rough part of town. He taught a computer technician program. His students were people with criminal records or gang affiliations, homeless or domestic violence victims. When one of his students would place in a good job, I would watch his face light up as he shared their success. He was making a difference, and he was happy at their success. His focus was not just teaching the technical program but also on being present to a person grappling with many fears. My friend could not change his students' home environment, but he could show them the possibility of a different life where peace was possible.

In my work as a healing arts practitioner, I would often hear questions about purpose. What is my purpose? Why am I here? What am I supposed to be doing with my life? I know I should be doing something else, but what? The clients that asked these questions felt their lives had no meaningful direction. Some of the clients felt an inner restlessness. Some clients felt disempowered to make the changes needed to take control of their peace. They often felt like nothing they did makes a difference. They felt their work to be dry and uninspiring. These clients would describe feeling lost and empty. Feeling lost and empty is a symptom of the wounded creative core.* Feeling lost and empty is the gap between living in compliance with institutional rules and your heart-soul wisdom. You suppress your inner need to create when you submit and conform to institutions. The heart's needs are lost to the machine of 'civilization.' The heart numbs itself to keep from feeling the continual hurt. Heart numbness becomes emptiness. When you comply with institutional mores, trauma stops the flow of life force energy. The heart looks for ways to express itself, and in institutional subjugation, there is often only more trauma.

The Wounded Creative Core is described in an essay available on the Emotional Patterns website emotionalpatterns.com/wounded-creative-core/ and a video and essay on remen-q.com/wounded-creative-core/.

You block purpose when you are attached to identity. An attachment to an identity can cause the heart to be numb. When you are attached to an identity, you are unwilling to let go. You create an identity to protect your beliefs and patterns that keep you safe. For example, George is a construction contractor, and he feels his work is drudgery. He describes his job as grinding away his soul. George needs his father's approval and love, so he went to work in his father's construction business. When he goes home, he is tired, and his fatigue does not allow him to be present to his family. He feels a strong pull to spend more time with his wife and children. George's heart is whispering that his purpose is to create heart connections to his family. His heart longs to be a more present parent and husband, his purpose. The identity he has created does not allow him to cut back on his family business time. He is not allowing himself joy or his purpose. He is holding onto an identity that keeps him from being aligned with the yearnings of his heart. He is living an old belief that doing what gives him joy will not pay the bills. He is living a belief that he has to give everything to the business to have his father's love and approval. He has conformed and complied with the familial institution. It is a safe projection that if George continues doing this job for many more years, he will develop a physical malady anchored in not allowing himself joy and denying his heart's yearning. George's woundedness is rooted in his ancestry. George's ancestors experienced severe deprivation and found that the only way to survive was to work hard and support the family business at all costs.

It is through the heart that your soul speaks to you.

A lack of gratitude blocks purpose. Gratitude is a way of acknowledging within yourself the flow of life. When there is a lack of gratitude, you live unconsciously - you are not present in the moment. Living unconsciously is living the life scripted by the religious, familial, educational, and government institutions. You live in fear of not meeting the institutional rules, not paying the bills, not being good enough, not meeting expectations, having sinned, etc.

Frees Up Energy

The Remen Q̄ process frees up the life energy you have been using to keep life-killing concepts energized (worry, anger, revenge, resentment, jealousy, worthlessness, chaos, etc.). To be in a state of non-peace requires focusing life force energy to maintain the non-peace. For example, worry causes your heart to contract; your thoughts are projecting into the future about what might happen. You might have also caused an uncomfortable contraction in your tummy, given yourself a headache, and your neck becomes tight and hurts. That is a lot of energy focused on a future based on fear. If you are not worrying and are present in the primacy of the moment, you are using that freed-up energy to focus on what needs to be done. Once you have released the past and stop trying to control the future, you become free. You are free to be in the present. Life energy begins to flow more freely in the present. Instead of feeling drained, distracted, and exhausted, you are present and have a renewed energy level. You now have a flow of life energy that can be applied to exercise, being alone, being present with others, serving your community, meditation, reading, cooking a healthy meal, a creative project, etc.

Wellness

When you use Remen $\overline{Q}$ to bring your heart to a state of peace, you create a feeling of wellness. Wellness is defined as a general sense of well-being. Well-being is how you perceive your physical health and your mind's state; it is about the whole ecosystem. When there is flow, no resistance, you feel at peace; you feel a sense of well-being. Wellness is not just about you; it is about the reality you create. It is not just "I feel good; therefore, I am experiencing wellness." Wellness is about the whole ecosystem of relationships. Wellness is an awareness of oneness, our interconnectedness to the natural world. When you experience wellness, you live and act without regard to the ego; there is a harmony between body, heart, and thinking minds. Harmony allows for joy and more peace.

Wellness starts with an awareness of what your heart is feeling. Wellness requires that you be present to the feeling in your heart. You may have numbed your heart to survive the pain you felt from hurtful events. You know you have numbed your heart when you experience repeated patterns of non-peace and cannot identify an associated heart contraction. For example, you are in a relationship that does not respect your needs. Instead of consciously responding to the disrespect, you numb your heart and do nothing. You do not allow yourself to feel the emotions of disrespect. Creating a peace hygiene practice creates the space for wellness and transmutes relationships of non-peace to peace.

With Remen Q̄ you develop a heightened awareness of what you have created that does not sustain life; that stops the flow of life force. When we restrict the flow of energy through the illusion of an out-of-balance identity, we create dis-ease. We create a degrading system of health. When life energy is constricted, bodily systems begin to break down. They function in ways that abandon their nature and support the creation of imbalances. For example, Tom, a computer analyst, believes that he is not allowed to have joy. He has lived his life working hard and doing his duty to the point of inner destruction. He begins to feel fatigued, reduced flow of life force, and in time he finds that his pancreatic function has declined in response to not allowing himself to experience joy.

Wellness of the heart, peace, is wellness of the body.

Kibriya

The word 'kibriya' is the term used by Rumi to describe the ecstasy of the divine. The heart is your connection to kibriya. Kibriya is the actualization of a connection between your heart and your divine nature. As you strip away the layers of attachment and fears, you may experience a joyous ecstasy, kibriya. Kibriya arises from a heart that is free of the created illusion of fear. Kibriya is your natural state. Kibriya is the wild, boundless, and unfettered flow of divine energy. Kibriya enters the heart and spreads to your whole being. There is no matrix of rules that define the experience of kibriya. When you are at peace, you move beyond the need to hold your suffering out to the world. If you choose to see your journey as a glorious experience of the soul, the Remen $\bar{Q}$ Method will bring you to a state of kibriya, divine grace, and ecstasy.

One day I had done my morning meditation, and a feeling of non-peace arose in my consciousness. I did the Remen $\bar{Q}$ process and then spent the morning in bliss, dancing in the kitchen and down the hallways as I did my household chores. I was drunk on the ecstasy of the divine. I was experiencing a state of bliss.

So often I put up my hands
To shield my eyes from you
Wild hilarious miracle!
Your Light shines through my bones.
~Rumi

Our heart centers have been imprisoned by the government, corporations, cultural mores, media messages, religious dogmas, family rules, education mandates and ancestral traumas based on attachment. This imprisonment is intentional. A controlling entity can leverage power, control, and profit over a population fearful of losing an identity, money, a job, and possessions. If you are afraid to lose something, it is an attachment. Attachments create the illusion of belonging within the institutions. Your fear keeps those attachments in place. When you comply with the rules to keep an attachment, you have temporarily closed yourself to the experience of your divine nature, kibriya. If you fear losing your job, you will do what a corporation tells you to do. If you fear losing your family's acceptance, you will behave in a way that aligns with their values. If your family and culture place a high value on education, they will force that value on you at the expense of your well-being and individuality. Most religions enforce control through indoctrinated shame and humiliation, which is then implemented within the family and community.

All attachments will eventually degrade, which creates suffering. Suffering from the degradation of an attachment will create a pattern that becomes an aspect of a person's identity. For example, Barry is a dedicated software engineer. Barry works long hours for the software company that employs him. Barry has not adapted to new technologies, nor does he have the college degree required by his employer for all new employees. He has specific skills and is considered the go-to expert on a particular software. Barry's software company must hire the skills it needs to re-engineer and advance existing products. Barry is no longer required, and he is laid off. Barry becomes resentful of his past employer and gets stuck in his anger. His relationships become a place of non-peace with his attachment to what was in the past.

> *The root of suffering is attachment.*
> *~The Buddha*

Once you acknowledge your attachment patterns and how they were created to make you comply, you can begin to unravel the fear these dogmas, rules laid down by 'authority, have created within you. Then, when you own your states of non-peace, you can make conscious choices about shifting to peace.

Kibriya is freedom from the collectively created illusion of suffering and the attachment to that suffering. Kibriya is the experience of the lightness of being that comes from shifting created patterns of non-peace to peace. Kibriya is your experience of your heart's connection to the divine nature of love. Filters of confusion

and chaos are lifted from your heart, and the heart becomes pure awareness.

How is Remen Q̄ Different from Other Emotional Release Techniques?

The way to peace is through the whole.
Without a heart at peace, there is no whole.

Heart-Based

The Remen Q̄ Method is a four-step process based on the heart. Remen Q̄ is based on what your heart tells you. If your heart is contracted, then there is fear and incoherence; there is non-peace. The Remen Q̄ process uses the contraction in your heart to focus your intention. In the Remen Q̄ process, you are transforming the underlying beliefs, created patterns, emotional states, and traumas of your created pattern(s) into a potential for peace. Your focus is on attaining a peaceful heart.

Peace is an expansion of the heart, and non-peace is a contraction of the heart. Non-peace is held as exclusionary, closed, rigid, contracted and biased. You experience a contraction in your heart when an emotional pattern of non-peace arises in your awareness. Non-peace, when recognized by the thinking-mind, is then given a label of I am anxious, I am angry, I am depressed, I am sad, I am worried, etc. The body-mind feels anger, anxiety, sadness, depression, worry, etc. Non-peace is separation and isolation. Peace is open, inclusive, neutral, and a flowing expansiveness. Peace is experienced as a state of oneness. When recognized by the thinking-mind, peace is given a label of overall wellness; I am at peace, I feel calm, etc.

Do-It-Yourself

Remen Q̄ is a do-it-yourself process. If your heart hurts and you are done with feeling contracted, use the Remen Q̄ process. Does your heart still feel contracted? If the answer is no, you are done. If yes, repeat the Remen Q̄ process.

In the moment of non-peace, you can shift your reality to peace. You do not need to wait for an appointment with an emotional release practitioner. You do not need to attend days of training. However, you may feel like you need to watch an instruction video or practice a few times to feel like you've mastered the process.

Whenever I experience a heart contraction, I don't wait to be in a private space to do the Remen Q̄ process. I close my eyes for a few moments and do the Remen Q̄ process. However, if you experience non-peace while driving, please wait until you are in a safe place. *

Anecdotally, I am aware of Remen Q̄ done with the eyes open.

No Bypass

A bypass is a state where you believe you have re-leased or cleared a state of non-peace and later dis-cover that the change was temporary. If doing Remen $\overline{Q}$ has not transmuted the relationship of non-peace, the state of non-peace will return. For example, you believe 'I am not good enough.' Perhaps you have used an emo-tional release technique to <u>replace</u> that created pattern with 'I'm good enough.' You believe that the created pat-tern has cleared, and then you discover that it returns the next time a trigger for 'not being good enough' is en-countered. You may feel let down, disappointed, angry, betrayed, and untrusting if you have experienced a by-pass. A bypass does not get to the underlying trauma that created the limiting pattern. A bypass does not get to the multiple traumas that are part of your experience of a limiting pattern. A bypass will divert you from your inner work. A bypass may cause a person to be deceived into thinking that they can stop ongoing medical care. A bypass may mask symptoms of a serious chronic dis-ease, thus causing a delay in treatment.

The state of peace that you achieve with the Remen $\overline{Q}$ process is for the experience of non-peace you are feeling at that moment. That moment, that trigger, and that pattern hold a unique vibration.

You have to do the 'work' of resolving limiting emo-tional patterns. You have to own the aspect of your identity that created the limiting pattern, even if the source is an ancestor. You may have success with Remen $\bar{Q}$. You have felt that feeling of peace, and you go about your life. Remen $\bar{Q}$ is as much a process as it is a singular event. I have been steadfastly working with Remen $\bar{Q}$ for over four years. It is 'a way'. As I work on my states of non-peace, I am changing. I am reaching the sweet state of bliss on a more frequent basis. I can invoke the feeling of bliss. I feel more present in all of the moments of my life. My decisions are conscious. **Remen $\bar{Q}$ is part of a journey, not a trip to the mini-mart**. I recommend that you read the Wikipedia article on Spiritual Bypass[16]. The article references several publications that explain bypasses.

Remen $\bar{Q}$ does not clear a specifically created pattern to be replaced with another created pattern. For example, you experience not feeling good enough. Your heart contracts and you enter a state of non-peace. In that state of non-peace, you may experience shame, humiliation, and wanting to hide. There are many patterns of non-peace within this one experience. With Remen $\bar{Q}$ you set the intention for peace, and after doing the Remen $\bar{Q}$ process, maybe multiple times, you feel calm and neutral. The feeling of not being good enough, shame, humiliation, and wanting to hide has been changed to the possibility that has the highest probability at that moment for peace.

You may find that in the future, you may need to address a feeling of non-peace again. That feeling may have the same label, but it is not the same created pattern transmuted in the past. Starting a practice or 'a way' of self-reflection, journaling, meditation, and using Remen $\overline{Q}$ are helpful in the journey to peaceful awareness. This practice offers you the opportunity to explore the non-peace that has not yet risen into your conscious awareness.

Story. In the early 2000's I attended an introductory workshop that demonstrated the use of a modality. The founder called a volunteer to the front of the auditorium and used the modality on the volunteer. The man's severe physical issue shifted before my eyes. I was so impressed I took three courses from this person. Later, I discovered that the man's physical problem had reverted to its previous state within a few days. This man's shift was a bypass **–the end**.

Gentle

Remen Q̄ does not need the details or source of a created pattern to create peace. You do not need to know the origin of the non-peace. You are merely witnessing what arises in your inner vision. The image may be symbolic, and the image can be pretended. Forcing yourself to access traumatic memories can cause more traumas. I have worked with clients where the source of the trauma was obscured from their memories. These clients would get frustrated when they could not access that information. This frustration and identification with frustration would sabotage the process. Remen Q̄ does not ask you to find that information; it transmutes it without the specifics.

If a heart contraction results from a state of non-peace, that contraction will exist in the thinking-mind, heart-mind, and body-mind. When this contraction is relaxed, you return to your natural state of peace after allowing peace with Remen Q̄.

Part 3: The Knowing Heart

Knowing

Your heart is much more than just a muscle pumping blood. Your heart is an energetic center with a bridge to the wisdom of the soul. The first organ to develop in your body is the heart[8]; your heart has an intuitive sense of knowing in a state of peace. Your heart is a center of consciousness that sends and receives information to the thinking-mind and body-mind. Your heart is the sender and receiver of information to others. Your heart differentiates between peace and non-peace feelings. Your heart is the seat of the experience of 'kibriya.'

The heart is an aspect of the soul manifested into form. At conception, there is a mergence of two strands of DNA, and at that moment, the connection to your animating life force, the primal heart, is created. The primal heart develops into the heart organ. You access inspired or transcendent thought through the heart-to-soul wisdom. This is an altered state of consciousness that is an extra-dimensional experience of awareness. Your experience of this oneness is through a heart at peace. A heart at peace is open to transcendent knowing, a knowing sourced from beyond the thinking-mind's logic. The heart in a state of peace embodies the expansive and inclusive nature of your humanity; compassion, love, joy, kindness, and hope. A heart in a state of non-peace is blocked to the experience of transcendent awareness and

feels contracted. Feelings in the heart that create contraction and exclusion are anger, betrayal, greed, jealousy, worry, sadness, defeat, worthlessness, hatred, etc.

Knowing is the feeling you get from the Soul.

**The heart is not just the inflow and outflow of blood
caused by its pumping action; it is also the sender
and receiver of knowing**. The heart is a portal to knowing from the soul. Knowing is an awareness in your
consciousness. Knowing is information that is sourced
from oneness. Through the heart, you access knowing
that will bring you peace. When your heart has a knowing, the wisdom comes through the heart and informs the
thinking-mind, which informs the body-mind. Knowing
is peace in your actions; there is no incoherence. Knowing is understanding. Knowing is information not derived from logical, analytical thinking processes. Knowing is wisdom derived from an awareness of the soul.
Knowing is a subtle awareness of events and how they
will unfold. Knowing is a deep sense that your actions
are in alignment with being in a state of peace. Have
you ever been to a social gathering, and you get a sense
of unease? You get a sense that you need not be part of
what is happening in this space, and then when you
leave, there is a sense of peace in your heart. You have
trusted that knowing and returned to a state of peace.

Story. A friend of mine was looking for a place to live.
She answered an ad for living arrangements that includ-
ed a little house in exchange for doing a few chores. My

friend made an appointment for a meeting with the person who placed the ad. The day before the meeting, I spoke with my friend. She said she had a bad feeling about this meeting and was thinking of canceling. She trusted that feeling and canceled the meeting. She received a bizarre email in response to her cancellation, indicating that the person represented an oppressive cult. Trusting the knowing in her heart saved my friend certain difficulty—**the end**.

Heart as a Guide

When you focus your awareness on your heart in a state of peace and ask a question, you will receive an answer. The heart must be at peace to transmit information that your thinking-mind can then receive. You are sometimes faced with choices or decisions that seem difficult. Choices or decisions are only problematic if there is incoherence in the minds (heart, body, and thinking). Incoherence is when at least one of your three minds is experiencing something different than the other minds.

When you are incoherent, you can quickly move yourself to a place of coherence. You do this by closing your eyes, touching your heart with your fingertips, or placing the open palm of your hand over your heart. Then, breathe through your nose softly and slowly for a few breaths while keeping your awareness on your heart. This simple exercise quiets the incoherence in the minds and takes only a few seconds to do. This breathing exercise will calm your heart and the other minds long enough for you to ask a question of your heart. The heart then speaks to the soul, and the soul whispers back. That answer will bring you a knowing of what is needed.

Story: I recently bought a replacement car for the car we towed behind our recreational vehicle. When I finalized the purchase details, the finance person asked me if I would like to buy the repair warranty. I told him to give me a moment. I did a breathing exercise and asked my inner self if this would be a purchase of value for me. I heard "no." So I told the finance person that I would pass on the repair warranty. He then pushed and asked, "Are you sure?" He then lowered the price of the repair warranty by $600. Before saying "yes" to his offer, I checked in again and heard, "this would be a wise choice"**--the end.**

Feelings

The heart sends feelings out to the body. The thinking-mind will label a feeling experience. The body then emotes; creates an action. For example, a feeling of embarrassment may cause a person's face to flush or turn red. A feeling that something is wrong may cause a contraction in the body's midsection (stomach or intestines). A feeling of love creates a series of biological reactions that yield a sense of overall well-being. A feeling of joy may create smiling, dancing, and laughter. These feelings are first felt by the heart, then identified by the body's thinking mind and emoted.

Deeper Understanding of Self

The deeper understanding of self lies in the heart. You are the expression of your heart. When your heart is neutral, calm and at peace, your interactions and relationships reflect that reality. When your heart is contracted, you are expressing your non-peace in your relationships. Your heart tells you that you are experiencing an aspect of self that reflects your non-peace or trauma in this relationship. Your heart becomes your teacher and guide for higher learning in that moment of contraction. By acknowledging the contraction, you also acknowledge that you own this state of non-peace. The contraction in your heart is yours to hold onto or change to peace.

If you ask your heart, it will show the patterns of suffering that you create. When your heart suffers, it is the soul's red light that says stop and look at what you have as a pattern. The suffering created by a heart's contraction is the pain that may move you to seek peace if you make that choice.

The heart knows the deeper understanding underlying the motivations of your actions. In your relationships, you not only have experiences that create spiritual, mental, and emotional growth for yourself, but you contribute to the spiritual, mental, and emotional development of others. By connecting to this awareness, you can make a conscious choice to experience non-peace in a relationship, or you can use Remen Q̄ to change the non-peace to peace. For example, if you keep repeating situations of failure in life, the heart knows that you need to learn to love yourself and transmute the wounds of feeling unloved and unwanted.

Story. A friend had just bought a used car from a dealer. She had a warranty on the vehicle, and two weeks into owning the car, the thermostat failed. The warranty contract had a $200 deductible. The repair service gave her a quote that reflected the $200 deductible she would owe. The unexpected expense caused enormous stress. She had been working with Remen Q̄ randomly for several months. She did the Remen Q̄ process on the heart feelings related to the car repair. When she got the bill, she was not charged for the deductible or the repair. But, what followed is the real story. When she called to tell me about her experience, she began doing a mind dump of the patterns in her life limiting her. As she tracked back in her life, she found the repeating patterns causing her stress now had happened many times in her past. She had come to a deeper understanding of the role she had been playing in the chaos and drama of her life—**the end.**

Coherence

The minds are coherent when there is a sense of one-ness in the heart, thinking, and body-minds. Each of these minds has awareness and a specific focus. The body-mind is about your survival and safety. If you are in danger, the body-mind triggers an instinctual response. The heart-mind is the connection to knowing and the infinite wisdom of the soul. The heart-mind is our awareness of peace and connectedness. The thinking-mind is the center for logical thoughts. Incoherence and stress result when your three minds are each responding to information differently. When working in a large corporation, I worked at a very demanding job, and I was under the constant stress of reconciling the three different minds' incoherent demands. My thinking-mind was demanding that I meet my job responsibilities with better than average performances. My heart-mind yearned to be home with my children. My body-mind was scared that I would lose my ability to support and keep my children if I didn't do the work of two people.

Happiness is when what you think, what you say,
and what you do are in harmony.
~Mahatma Gandhi

Heart coherence is an energetic state of flow that connects you to infinite wisdom. When the heart is at peace, it strengthens the coherency to the body and thinking minds by entrainment. Entrainment happens when the body and thinking minds synchronize with calm and peace in the heart. As the states of non-peace change to peace in the heart with Remen $\bar{Q}$, the minds become unified, which creates a 'way' of peace and calm. The noise of the thinking and body-mind becomes quiet.

By being at peace, you are living in flow. The noise of the thinking mind does not control your heart. Problems are solved without resistance. While I was in college, a challenging problem was assigned. My study partner and I arranged to meet with one of the graduate students to solve the problem. I suddenly had this feeling of peace and knowing wash over my being. I 'knew' the answer. I went to the whiteboard and laid out the solution details. My thinking-mind had no idea what was going to flow onto the whiteboard as it was being written. The solution flowed from the heart's connection to universal wisdom.

> *Peace comes from within. Do not seek it without.*
> *~ Buddha*

When the wisdom of peace and coherence flows through the heart, it brings peace to others. Coherence is experienced as a sense of overall wellness of being. People will seek out others that allow them to experience that sense of peace within themselves. A coherent peaceful heart is inclusive. There is an openness to help others and practice compassion. The transcendent knowing that is felt within your heart does not stop at the edges of your chest. This knowing is a state of presence

89

and flow that has no agenda and no contraction. I have been to meditation classes where attendees will enter the meditation state within moments of closing their eyes. This rapid transition to a meditation state reflects entrainment to a heart's vibration at peace held by the meditation teacher.

When you do things from your soul, you
feel a river moving in you, a joy.
~Rumi

The experience of peace within the heart is a powerful impetus for shifting reality from a state of non-peace to peace. The experience of peace allows the feeling of joy, happiness, inspiration and laughter to enter without limits. That experience of peace within shows you that you had been living in opposition to your true nature.

Incoherence, non-peace, stops you from accessing the flow of heart-soul wisdom. The heart contraction caused by non-peace will stop the flow of coherent information; it will stop the heart-mind's flow of wisdom. The information experienced in a state of contraction comes from created patterns that are the result of trauma. Your responses, when you have a contracted heart, are reactive. Reactive responses can be a form of weak boundary. For example, a reactive response would be using confusion, overwhelm, or even anger to not deal with a challenging situation. A friend of mine was bullied in school. He would go into confusion and overwhelm anytime a relationship became slightly difficult. He would then shut down his emotions and run away from the relationship.   His projection of possible trauma triggered his reactive response.

Living from the Heart

When your heart is at peace, you live from the heart.
Your heart guides your feelings and actions. You know
and trust the guidance you receive from your heart.
There is a deep sense that your actions are in alignment
with your higher purpose. You have an awareness of
having a choice. Your awareness does not begin in the
thinking-mind's duality; it starts with noticing the feelings in your heart. Your awareness will then ask the
questions of the heart and look at the choices from the
heart. When living from the heart, you are living from a
place of aliveness. There is a different quality to all of
your senses. You see beyond the colors and the struc-
tures around you. You know the energy of aliveness in
all that surrounds you. You look at a rock, and you don't
see a rock. You see everything that happened before the
rock was a rock. You see its energy, you see its dynamic
qualities, and you see it's not a hard immovable static
element of the universe. The rock is alive. You see that
nothing in the universe is dead. You know the connectedness to all.

Story: For several years, I had a small web design and
development business. In one of my last web design
commercial projects, a client sent me files with the design they wanted on their website. As I progressed into
the project, I had a feeling in my heart that the direction
was not going to have the desired outcome. The feeling
became so intense I could not work on the project any

92

longer without shifting the artistry. When I came from the heart and spoke to the client about my feelings, the website magic began. Living from the heart brought joy and a sense of wholeness to the project—**the end.**

If your heart is contracted in a state of non-peace, that contraction can be felt by those around you. For example, when you feel anger in your heart, the people around you can feel it before it is expressed. In those angry moments, you contract, and the relationship connections convey that anger. Your reality then reflects your anger to you. That feeling of anger sent out to your body and into the world can hurt those who perceive it, including yourself. That anger may not even be directed at them, but they feel it. The person sensing the anger may feel anxious or suddenly feel angry themselves. If there is trust in the heart's information flow, a person will recognize that the anger comes from outside them and remains unconnected to the anger.

When you live from the heart, you lose your ability to speak meaningless words. You would rather sit mute than engage in meaningless banter. Not speaking and not acting are based on the calmness of heart and spirit. Your conversations are connected to the heart from the heart. When you speak from the heart, there is a sense of connection, joy, and resonance. When you speak from the heart, there is a much grander picture of connections and purpose. You will find that your relationships have meaning in your life.

Additional notes*:*

*The interactions between the thinking (brain), body, and heart minds have a complex physiological foundation not explored in this book. The focus of this book is to explore how using Remen $\bar{Q}$ facilitates the shift from non-peace to peace.

**There are different intuitive centers within your being. Those intuitive centers are not explored in this book. The heart's knowing sense affects the heart's state of peace. Remen $\bar{Q}$ focuses on what is felt in the heart. If you experience intuitive information from another energetic center, it still affects the heart.

Part 4: Questions & Answers

Frequently Asked Questions

This chapter explores some of the questions I have gotten over the last couple of years.

1. Isn't non-peace and peace a judgment? Only if you make it a judgment. Non-peace is contraction. Non-peace obstructs the flow of life force. That is the nature of non-peace. Peace is expansion. Peace is an unobstructed flow. That is the nature of peace. An observation of an experience's nature is not a value of right, wrong, good, or evil. When you experience contraction, you may experience discomfort or pain. This contraction is information.

2. Can I do this process for others? Why would you? There are times when I have facilitated a person shifting from non-peace to peace. I have walked them through the process. A person must own the limiting created pattern. They must be willing to let go of the identity that is part of that limiting pattern. They must be willing to do the 'work' to move past patterns that create chaos and confusion. You can do this work for yourself. For example, a friend is having a hard time with a family situation. This situation causes you to feel concerned. You can do Remen $\bar{Q}$ on yourself for the feelings of non-peace.

3. How do I shift my perception of reality when it feels like everything has come crashing down? Your awareness in a moment of chaos and pain is probably anxious and filled with a sense of confusion and overwhelm. In this experience, you are not thinking about possibilities and resources. You are reacting from a place of survival and safety. Your breath becomes the key to shifting yourself from panic and overwhelm. At this moment, touch your heart, bring your awareness to the space under your fingertips. There is a possibility that the pain of panic or anxiety grips the area under your fingertips. Slowly breathe through your nose until you feel a slight calming and then do a Remen $\bar{Q}$ process. Repeat the Remen $\bar{Q}$ process until there is peace. If this is not possible, ask a friend to help you reclaim your peace. Have the friend walk you through the breathing and the Remen $\bar{Q}$ process.

Story. A few years ago, two people I love deeply experienced a very dark place in their lives. Projecting into the future, I could see the possibility where both of them would no longer have a physical presence in my life. I had a melt-down. All I could think about was the loss of love and companionship I have always felt from these two people. Without them, I would feel very alone. I sat in my car in the Trader Joe's parking lot, a grocery store in the United States, crying and feeling helpless. My reactive mind said that there was nothing I could do. Then a small voice said, 'take back your peace.' I allowed myself to breathe into presence (touch your heart with your hand, moving your awareness to your heart, and taking five deep long breaths through the nose), and then I did the Remen $\bar{Q}$ process. I continued doing the Remen $\bar{Q}$ Method until my heart was no longer contracted, and it was filled with peace. In the next few days, both of these people had shifted direction—**the end.**

4. I can't feel or listen to my heart; how can I do Remen $\bar{Q}$? When you disconnect from your heart, you create heart deafness or numbness. Numbness or disconnection is not peace. You disconnected because you had an experience of heart pain that was overwhelming. You do not want to have that level of pain again. When you numb out or disconnect, you are pushing an experience's emotional pain into your body. Below are three possible approaches to using Remen $\bar{Q}$ to reclaim feeling in your heart center:

i. If you are aware that you are deaf to your heart's messages, you are aware of the numbness. Use Remen $\bar{Q}$ to transmute the numbness and disconnection by focusing on the numbness as the place of non-peace. Do Remen $\bar{Q}$ until the numbness is no longer there and you feel complete.

ii. Do a scan of your body. Where do you feel the pain of your heart numbness? You may have several places in your body that hold the pain. Start with the one place that holds the most intensity at this moment. Use that as your place of non-peace, then do Remen $\bar{Q}$. Continue using Remen $\bar{Q}$ until the pain has lessened or neutralized. Now check your heart.

What are you aware of now? Does it feel expansive and peaceful? If not, do more Remen Q̄ until you feel complete.

iii. Use reflective meditation with the heart deafness/numbness as your focus. Then use Remen Q̄ to transmute what arises in your meditation.*

*The process of reflective meditation is described in #8 below.

5. I can't visualize. I don't see anything in my inner vision. What am I doing wrong? It could be that your dominant method of processing information is either kinesthetic or auditory. If you are kinesthetic, your origin representation may involve feelings or movement. If you are auditory, your origin representation may be voices, music, or other sounds. You will experience the origin representation according to your dominant method of accessing information.

6. What about chakras and the emotional content held there? If you have emotional content that creates non-peace in a chakra, you still feel it in your heart. For example, you are feeling judged by someone in your life. The throat chakra is affected by judgment. A feeling of being judged may result in neck, throat, thyroid, or larynx issues. That feeling of being judged is still experienced in the heart.

7. Does Remen Q̄ need to be done more than once on a created pattern? Yes and no. I have found that sometimes a pattern will shift with doing the process once. I have also found that multiple patterns may have been triggered, and then I will do the process numerous times. Always go back to your heart and feel. Is it now in a state of peace or still a feeling of contraction? If there is still contraction, then there is a need to do additional Remen Q̄ processes. The number of repetitions will vary with each person. Sometimes there is a need to experience the created pattern in layers. Long-standing created patterns have layers. Each layer is unique; it has a historical reference and vibration different from every other experience of the created pattern.

Story. A relative had a sequence of events unfold that was going to create chaos. I felt my heart contract around this state of non-peace. I did several Remen Q̄ sessions around my state of non-peace. I then had a sleep cycle, and I did more the next day. The state of non-peace shifted to peace for my relative and me—**the end.***

Anecdote: If the state of non-peace is a relationship to relatives, then more layers of created patterns may be present, resulting in the need to do more than one or two Remen Q̄ exercises.

8. Will the changes last? You must pay attention to your heart. Your heart will tell you when it is complete. Immediately after completing a Remen Q̄ exercise, you will want to re-check your heart. If you feel a contraction in your heart, re-do the Remen $\bar{Q}$ process until it feels complete. The intensity of a remaining heart contraction may be very subtle. If there is no sense of peace, then do the Remen $\bar{Q}$ exercise again.

Use journaling or reflective meditation to explore similar patterns or events that create non-peace as part of an active approach to your personal transformation work.

Journaling allows you to focus on the questions that arise at that moment. A question may arise, and then it is replaced by another thought. When you journal, you become your listener; you become present to your heart's transmission of whispers from the soul. Journaling allows you to explore your feelings without judgment. Journaling allows you to change as you are writing (It is journaling's gift). As you write, you are listening with your heart. You may have learned not to listen to your heart. You may have learned that you cannot trust your heart. Remen $\bar{Q}$ any heart contraction that comes up around trusting yourself or knowing your heart's information.

As I journal, patterns of non-peace will arise in my awareness. I will write it down, do the Remen $\bar{Q}$ process, and check-in with my heart. If there is still a contraction, I will repeat the process until I feel neutral.

Reflective meditation is a form of meditation where you focus on a subject (My teachers used to call this

101

daydreaming.). Give yourself some quiet space as if you were going to meditate or pray. You set the intention of bringing into your awareness the patterns of non-peace that are the subject of your focus. You allow the focus of your query to flow. You are not directing the flow; you are allowing. As you become aware of other non-peace patterns, use the Remen $\bar{Q}$ process until you feel complete. The contraction you experience in doing this process with reflective meditation may be very subtle. The contraction may also come as an ache or another form of physical discomfort in your body.

What may have felt like or appeared to be the same created pattern, in essence, is different. **A created pattern may have several secondary created patterns.** For example, you may have a created pattern of not feeling good enough. You have struggled with that limiting pattern most of your life. Each time you experienced not being good enough, there was a different time, place, reference experience and maybe other people. The created pattern may be 'I'm not good at drawing.'; 'I'm not good at cooking.'; 'I'm not good enough for promotion.'; 'I'm not good enough to be loved.'; and so on. You only know that you feel not good enough. Each one of these examples is a different created pattern. With Remen $\bar{Q}$ you will address the 'not good enough' pattern present in the moment. If you practice Remen $\bar{Q}$ as a 'way' and journal, these limiting patterns will show themselves, and you can change them to peace. When I meditate, I will sometimes get a visual of an experience that created a limiting pattern. I will then use Remen $\overline{Q}$ to create peace.

9. I have done the Remen $\overline{Q}$ on a situation in my life. I feel peace in my heart, but there was a recent event of trauma-drama in this situation. Can I Remen $\overline{Q}$ future possibilities? Yes. I have a friend with an adult child that was in an unsafe situation. My friend's physical health deteriorated, and she was on multiple medications because of the stress caused by this situation. My friend did the Remen $\overline{Q}$ on herself. She was able to reach a place of calm and go off the medication. A few weeks later, she did the Remen $\overline{Q}$ process again when there was another episode of trauma-drama, even though she was at peace with what had happened. When visualizing the origin, the inner vision, she felt she was witnessing a future probability. The reality she shifted was her own.

10. Do I need to identify the created pattern? No. You have already framed the created pattern(s) by acknowledging a pattern of repeated events or feelings. By embracing the actual events representing the patterns, instead of identifying the created pattern(s), you allow for the possible shift of multiple created patterns. Example: A person has problems staying in housing. The housing insecurity issues seem to just happen to them. They have to move again and again. They can't get settled in one place before they have to move again. This person experiences a great deal of expense, angst, and insecurity with each move. The need to move may be several created patterns. The created patterns may be 'I don't feel safe when I stay in one place for long.'; 'I need to move before someone kicks me out. '; 'I'm not good enough to stay in one place.'; 'I'm not good enough to have a home.'; 'Bad things always happen to me. '; 'If I stay in one place, someone will hurt me.'; and so on. This person would then use the Remen $\bar{Q}$ process on the most recent event. Once that is clear, they could then remember the other events of housing insecurity and see if there is a contraction around those events.

11. Some people have tried so many different approaches and modalities that they become vested in the idea that nothing will ever work. There is a possibility that someone with this experience holds a victim identity and victim thinking. **Will Remen $\bar{Q}$ work for those people?** No. It will only work if they are willing to let go of their victim identity and victim thinking. They must own what happens to them. They can use Remen $\bar{Q}$ to transmute the victim identity and thinking.

12. What is the difference between kibriya and enlightenment? Kibriya is a heart awareness of peace. It is a state of no desire, and you will have everything you need. There is a complete alignment of the masculine and feminine in the heart. It is your natural state. Enlightenment is a higher consciousness state with an awareness of the cosmic self.

13. Can anger be transmuted with Remen $\bar{Q}$? Yes. When you approach any created pattern and anger is a

104

repeating pattern, you do so with mindfulness. You are very aware of the lack of peace in your being. You feel the contraction in your heart. The softening that comes from mindful breath sets the field of intention to peace. Use the 'breathing into presence' exercise before moving into a Remen $\overline{Q}$ exercise.

14. If someone is angry at me, how is their anger mine? You have created a reality where they are angry at you. The reality is yours, and if you are feeling their anger, it is also your anger. When you change your heart from non-peace to peace, you no longer feel their anger. You are no longer contributing energy to the anger relationship. Your shift to peace does not mean that they aren't still angry. It means that you are not contributing a relationship of anger to their state of non-peace.

15. Can you Remen $\overline{Q}$ energetic connections? Yes. Energetic connections are relationships. You have a relationship with everyone you know and don't know. You have relationships with relatives, friends, the clerk at the grocery store, medical support personnel, everyone. With some people, you have multiple types of relationships. For example, a person can have a friend that is a relative, and that relative is also a business partner. Each of those roles is a relationship with different qualities. Relationships can be joyous, neutral, or create feelings of contraction.

How a relationship affects us depends on the quality of the relationship. If the relationship is genuine, supportive, and fun, then you are energized by the connection. There is a flow of energy in the relationship. If the relationship is one where one person can only receive, then the other person will feel exhausted when around this person. An out-of-balance relationship is a relationship that does not create peace. The lack of peace and the lack of flow is based on your state of non-peace. The other person in the relationship is mirroring your emotional state that is creating non-peace.

Story. I walked into my partner's office to help with a computer issue, and he told me he had received a phone call from a client. The client could not tell him everything he needed to say and told him he would call him back. I immediately had a heart contraction and a feeling of fear I could not shake. I went back to my office and sat for a moment. I asked the question, 'what am I feeling?' I heard 'my partner's concern.' I was feeling a reflection of my fear. I did a Remen $\bar{Q}$ process. It took a couple of passes at the Remen $\bar{Q}$ process before my heart space became calm and neutral. This event triggered the childhood fear of the unknown—**the end.**

16. What about Karma? Karma is memory. You create your reality from your memory. Remen $\bar{Q}$ transmutes the limiting created patterns that are the product of memory.

17. How does prayer compare to Remen $\bar{Q}$? Some types of prayer pray for the granting of a specific outcome. Praying for a particular result is praying-your-fear. You are creating the very thing that you do not want. With Remen $\bar{Q}$ you set the intention for peace, enter a state of presence, and then you witness a representation of the origin of the non-peace. You're thoughts (mind), feelings (heart), and emotions (body) are in alignment. With Remen $\bar{Q}$ you are not defining an outcome. The change in your reality when shifting from non-peace to peace will be the most probable of the possible outcomes.

For example, a friend's daughter is seriously ill and may die. You feel grief, and your heart contracts with fear that this may happen. Your beliefs bring you to pray for this person's recovery. Your prayers are coming from grief and fear. Before you start praying, use Remen $\bar{Q}$ to create a state of peace within yourself. Then your prayers will be from peace and an intention of peace.

18. Can I use this procedure in an altered state produced by herbs, sugar, alcohol, or pharmaceuticals?
Any artificially induced mental condition that prevents you from being fully present and aware of the sensations in your body will inhibit you from transmuting non-peace to peace. Herbs, sugar, alcohol, or pharmaceuticals that alter awareness, change the chemistry in your body. That change to your body chemistry will change your ability to feel the pattern and visualize it. Remen $\bar{Q}$ is a do-it-yourself process, but for some people, it is not possible to discontinue the use of herbs or pharmaceuticals. In this scenario, another person willing to work

with the Remen $\overline{Q}$ method and owning the issue is a potential option.

This question was asked by someone on a medication that altered their ability to feel the non-peace. They were aware of the non-peace. In this case, I would offer that the person journal their awareness of the non-peace, do the Remen $\overline{Q}$ and then track their awareness of the non-peace through their journal. If the issue arises again, then repeat the journaling process with Remen $\overline{Q}$.

19. Will Remen $\overline{Q}$ change the current world condition from non-peace to peace? Yes. You can use Remen $\overline{Q}$ to alter your state of non-peace related to the world state to peace. Chaotic, erratic, or weak efforts get replaced with purpose, focus, and direction. Those are powerful forces for peace in even one person. The more people respond from a heart at peace, the more effective the change.

20. I feel lost in my journey to awareness; what should I do? Feeling lost can be a stuck trauma where freezing was the response. The feeling of lost can stop you from making choices or decisions. By staying frozen, not moving, you stay safe. You stay safe but also keep the feeling of frozen and lost. These are states of non-peace.

Once you have worked through the 'lost' feeling with Remen $\overline{Q}$ look at the possible options for engaging in your journey to awareness. I suggest meditation, classic

Yoga, Qigong, drumming journeys, bodywork, breathwork, Tai Chi, read the texts of ancient wisdom, study what you have read, and journal the reflections of your heart. Pay attention to how your heart feels and use Remen Q̄ to transmute the created patterns of non-peace when they appear. Go to a metaphysical bookstore or visit your local bookstore section that focuses on self-exploration or spirituality and cruise the aisles until you find a specific topic that quickens your pulse. Visit an introductory Yoga, Qigong, or Tai Chi session to see if you resonate with one of those forms of meditative movement. Many metaphysical bookstores will have classes that may be of interest. If you struggle with journaling, I suggest the book by Julia Cameron, The Artist's Way, or check your local metaphysical center for a journaling class. Bodywork and energy healing (reiki, healing touch, breathwork, massage, craniosacral therapy, reflexology, somatic bodywork, myofascial release, etc.) done with intention will bring created patterns you have buried to the surface of your awareness.

While on a journey of understanding, you may feel lost; you have consciously landed in the field of potentiality. I suggest you get comfortable in that space. If you find you feel fear in that space, then use Remen Q̄ to find your peace in the field of potentiality. The field of potentiality is where there are many paths available to you at that moment. I also suggest you get comfortable with change. Allow yourself to see with the eyes of a child. The universe is this fantastic place, and the wonder of a child opens you to the experiences it has to offer.

Alone Time

Spend time alone and learn to be present to yourself. Use this time for self-reflection and journal what arises in the silence. Be aware of what your body holds. We can develop inner deafness to the endless chatter of self-deprecating thoughts. These thoughts and physical discomforts are not harmless. They are states of non-peace. These thoughts build anxiety. If being alone feels fearful or anxious, use the Remen $\bar{Q}$ process to shift that state of non-peace to peace. I find silence to be a luxurious time of nurturing myself. I am genuinely excited to experience what the silence gives me. In that silence, there is never a feeling of being alone. I awake at around 4 a.m. most days to write, read, reflect on my heart and meditate.

Bodywork and Energy Healing

Bodywork and energy healing will bring created patterns into your awareness when buried under pain and reactive responses. If the issue is chronic stress, bodywork or energy healing will be palliative until you have neutralized the patterns that create your stress. I suggest that you allow yourself to be aware of any emotions that arise during these sessions. As soon as possible, do Remen $\bar{Q}$ and journal your insights. Some practitioners will ask you what you feel as they touch or move a specific part of your body. They bring your focus into the present and the emotional patterns you may be holding.

Journaling

Journal and reflect on what you have read and any wisdom that arises in the silence. Journal your inner experiences. I have kept a journal for the last 30+ years. My journal often became a record of insights into our nature shared in this book and Emotional Patterns[13].

Some people may have a fear that their journal pages could be discovered and read. If that is the case, destroy the pages when your writing is complete for the day. I would suggest that if you cannot trust that your journal is safe from prying eyes, you may want to look at what it means not to trust the people in your home.

Nature

Spend time in nature. Find a tree and sit under it. Sit by a running river or creek and meditate on those sounds. Take a walk in a forest, focusing on your feet. As you walk, notice what arises as you focus on your feet, fully present to the path. Allow yourself the joy that comes from being part of nature. Listen to what you hear from your inner voice in this connection with the outdoors. Take your journal and reflect on the messages from your inner voice.

Yoga, Tai Chi, Qigong

Yoga, Tai Chi, or Qigong (there are many others) are ancient practices of specified movements that balance the mind and body. When done with a trained instructor, these practices will facilitate the neutralization of devitalizing patterns that have created non-peace. These practices move you out of the monkey mind and into your body. You become present with the information your body is giving you. The most profound meditation state I have experienced was with a yoga movement in an instructor-led environment.

Breathwork

Breathwork focuses on the breath in a continuous process of breathing. Breathwork creates altered states of consciousness, deep relaxation, and beneficial physiological changes. After a breathwork session, there is an experience of universal oneness, mental clarity, and increased energy levels.

Drumming Journeys

Drumming journeys open you to seeing aspects of yourself that may have been obscured in your illusions. When you pull back the shroud of illusion, you open yourself to the possibility of transmuting old patterns of identity. This opening is an ancient technique for self-exploration that accesses the subconscious mind. I suggest you find a drumming journey guide, someone who has been trained in drumming and facilitating your inner exploration.

Listen to Your Heart

While on my journey, when I listened to my heart, I could move to the next level of understanding. Higher awareness began when I entered the wisdom of silence through the heart and listened to my heart-soul wisdom. For example, in the early 2000s, I took a Craniosacral Therapy course. I wasn't able to do the technique. The harder I tried, the more frustrated I became. Finally, I heard my inner voice say, "meditate." I put my hands on my partner in the practice session and entered a light meditation. I was then able to feel the subtle movements of cerebral spinal fluid.

21.When I do a Remen Q̄ process, my body feels a lightness or lightheadedness. What's happening? The lightness is the flow of energy that has been obstructed and is now moving in your body. Remen Q̄ creates an energetic release, a rebalancing of the energy flow in your being. Light-headedness is your body adjusting to the state of peace where there had been non-peace be-fore.* The lightness or lightheadedness, typically, will only last a few seconds. If experiencing these shifts cre-ates fear or a heart contraction, Remen Q̄ the fear and see what your experience of those shifts becomes.

Note: You may experience unfettered joy while doing laundry, washing dishes, balancing a spreadsheet, or writing snippets of code after doing a Remen Q̄ process.

22. How do boundaries contribute to chaos and anxi-ety? Boundaries of any kind are born out of fear. There are three types of boundary states:

- Weak boundaries – Moves their boundaries de-pending on the secondary gain or fear. They take a problem as their own to fix it.

- <u>Strong/Healthy boundaries</u> - Advice without acknowledgment and empathy may give a sense of being unengaged. A person with strong boundaries won't cross their identity-based boundaries to be compassionate. Strong boundaries are based on their need to protect themselves; a need to protect yourself is fear.
- <u>Boundlessness</u> - allows the other to access their internal wisdom.

An example of a weak boundary would be if a patient allows their doctor to prescribe something they know is unsuitable for them when there is a better, more benign option, but the doctor insists. The patient is fearful of contesting the doctor's authority. The patient has shut down their heart wisdom. In a few weeks, they are very ill from the prescribed medication with a new long-term illness.

Strong boundaries do not create chaos and anxiety in the same way that weak ones do. Using the example in the previous paragraph, the doctor has demonstrated a boundary that could be determined to be a strong boundary. The doctor's response has shut down the flow of communication and created chaos in the process. The patient's response with a strong or healthy boundary would explain that the drug they are prescribing would cause a secondary condition and not take it. At this point, the doctor and patient have reached an impasse.

Boundlessness, using the example of the doctor and patient, would have cooperatively explored other options. These options would have engaged the doctor and patient's concerns and found a solution that improved their condition without the possibility of a secondary condition arising. At the same time, the doctor's and patient's needs are being respected.

23. Can I set an intention other than peace? No. Setting an intention other than peace will not have the desired outcome. For example, you want a new car. Something is blocking you from going out and purchasing a new car. So you set an intention for a new car. What state of non-peace brought you to the desire for a new car? Address the non-peace that you feel in your heart. The desire for a new car may have many different vibrational qualities of non-peace held within it. When you do Remen $\bar{Q}$ you are bringing into your awareness a visual that holds the vibrational match to the non-peace you are holding. You may need to do several passes of Remen $\bar{Q}$ because there could be several diverse states of non-peace blocking you're acquiring a new car. When you set an intention for a new car, the focus is on the car, not the non-peace; therefore, you are transmuting nothing. The states that may be blocking you from getting the new car are not transmuted. Following this example, if you need a new vehicle because your other car is a place of non-peace, then address the non-peace until you feel calm and neutral. Then start to look at solutions to replace the old car.

24. Can I predetermine the origin? No. The process works when you allow flow. An origin visual may go back many generations to an event you had no way of knowing. The need to predetermine the origin is not trusting the process. I suggest you start with the lack of trust. Then bring in the state of non-peace that brought you to this place and allow the Remen $\overline{Q}$ process.

25. What is the difference between being present and presence? Presence is a field of awareness that may extend beyond the immediate five senses. Being present means you are aware of the moment without thinking of the past or future.

Presence has several meanings, but the definition above is what I am using within this book.

Part 5: About the Journey

About Valeria

Valeria Moore is an author and consciousness journeyer. She has studied with a wide variety of consciousness and personal development teachers. Valeria holds a degree in Computer and Information Sciences from the University of California at Santa Cruz. She has worked in a variety of roles in the technology sector.

Valeria was born and raised in the Ozarks and then spent her early adult years in California raising her two daughters. Valeria now lives in Oregon with her life partner, Mike. She enjoys gardening, painting, woodworking, kayaking, hiking, and creative sewing. Valeria is a grandmother to four grandchildren with whom she also enjoys arts and crafts, baking, sewing, and reading.

Valeria is the author of <u>Emotional Patterns: Emotional States and Created Patterns by Malady</u>[13]; this book builds on her previous book, <u>Healer Wisdom</u>. The <u>Emotional Patterns</u> book explores the emotional states, fears, and created patterns found in diseases and disorders. She has been studying emotional states since the early 2000s. She continues to develop the <u>Emotional Patterns</u> database of wisdom with frequent additions. Lately, she has also ventured into writing children's books with an environmental aspect. Several more children's books are being developed.

Videos, upcoming events, and news about Remen $\overline{Q}$ are available at remen-q.com. You can explore <u>Emotional Patterns</u>[13] at emotionalpatterns.com.

"Change yourself, and you have done your part in changing the world."

~Paramahansa Yogananda

References

1. Peace Pilgrim (1964). *Steps Toward Inner Peace*. Wikisource, WikiMedia Project. en.wikisource.org/ wiki/Steps_ Toward_Inner_Peace. Accessed 6 June 2021.

2. Pearce, Fred (2015, August 17). *Global Extinction Rates: Why Do Estimates Vary So Wildly?*. Yale School of Environment. e360.yale.edu/features/global_extinction _rates_why_do_estimates_vary_so_wildly. Accessed 6 June 2021.

3. NASA (2018, January 18 . Release 18-003). *Long-term warming trend continued in 2017: NASA, NOAA*. NASA. www.nasa.gov/press-release/long-term-warming-trend-continued-in-2017-nasa-noaa. Accessed 6 June 2021.

4. Insurance Information Institute (2021, April 4). *Facts + Statistics: Wildfires*. Insurance Information Institute. iii.org/fact-statistic/facts-statistics-wildfires. Accessed 6 June 2021.

5. World Health Organization(2018,February 1). *Drought*. World Health Organizationwww.who.int/health-topics/drought#tab=tab_1 . Accessed 8 June 2021.

6. Worland, Justin (2019, June 13). *The Leaders of These Sinking Countries Are Fighting to Stop Climate Change. Here's What the Rest of the World Can Learn.* Time. time.com/ longform/sinking-islands-climate-change/. Accessed 8 June 2021.

7. Congressional Research Services (2021, April 21). *Central American Migration: Root Causes and U.S. Policy*. Congressional Research Services. fas.org/sgp/crs/row/IF11151.pdf. Accessed 8 June 2021.

8. Wikipedia, *Heart Development.* Reference 3. en.wikipedia.org/wiki/Heart_development. Accessed 11 June 2021.

9. Merriam-Webster, *Transmute.* Merriam-Webster. www.merriam-webster.com/dictionary/transmute. Accessed 7 February 2021.

10. Townley, Nathan Z (2016), *Awakening Within the System: Evolution, not Revolution*, Seattle, Washington, USA; A Global Band of Light Book. p. 150,151.

11. McTaggart, Lynne (2008). *The Intention Experiment: Using Your Thoughts to Change Your Life and the World*. New York, New York, USA; Free Press. p. xvi, xxi.

12. Bradbury, Ray (1952). *A Sound of Thunder.* USA; Crowell-Collier Publishing Co.

13. Moore, Valeria (2019). *Emotional Patterns*. Keizer, Oregon, USA; Self-Published.

14. Stelter, Gretchen (2016, December 18.). *A Beginner's Guide to the 7 Chakras and Their Meanings*. Healthline.www.healthline.com/health/fitness-exercise/7-chakras._Accessed 6 June. 2021.

15. Brule, Dan (2018). *Just Breathe: Mastering Breathwork For Success In Life, Love, Business, And Beyond*. New York, New York, USA; Atria/Enliven Books

16. Wikipedia. *Spiritual Bypass.* Wikipedia. en.wikipedia.org/wiki/Spiritual_bypass. Retrieved 14 April 2021

Resources

I have read thousands of books and articles about spirituality, consciousness, and energy fields. While writing this book, I reread some of those books, and others became a new part of this journey. The wisdom in those books and articles became part of me. As I read the books and articles below, my understanding would evolve.

1. Bukkyo Dendo Kyokai (1984), *The Teachings of Buddha,* Tokyo, Japan: Bukkyo Dendo Kyokai Society.

2. Gibran, Kahlil (1951), *The Prophet*, New York, New York, USA: Alfred A. Knopf., Inc.

3. Elwood, Robert (1983), *Finding the Quiet Mind*, Wheaton, Illinois, USA: Theosophical Publishing House

4. Moore, Valeria (2019), *Emotional Patterns (previously Healer Wisdom)*, Keizer, Oregon, USA: Self Published.

5. Cameron, Julia (1992), *The Artist's Way*, New York, New York, USA: Penguin Putnam inc.

6. Ruiz M.D, Don Miguel and Mills, Janet (1997), *The Four Agreements: A Practical Guide to Personal Freedom (A Toltec Wisdom Book),* San Rafael, California, USA: Amber-Allen Publishing.

7. Rosen, Larry (2012), *iDisorder: Understanding Our Obsession with Technology and Overcoming Its Hold On Us*, New York, New York, USA: St. Martin's Press.

8. Childre, Doc, Martin, Howard, Rozman, Deborah, McCraty, Rollin (2016), *Heart Intelligence*, Cardiff, California, USA: Waterfront Press.

9. Choa Kok Sui, Master (2003), *The Spiritual Essence of Man*, Makati, Philippines; Institute for Inner Studies Publishing Foundation, LLC.

10. Townley, Nathan Z (2016), *Awakening Within the System: Evolution, not Revolution*, Seattle, Washington, USA; A Global Band of Light Book.

11. Tolle, Eckhart (2004), *The Power of Now: A Guide to Spiritual Enlightenment*, Novato, California, USA: New World Library.

12. Tolle, Eckhart (2003), *Stillness Speaks*, Novato, California, USA: New World Library.

13. Bartlet, Richard (2007), *Matrix Energetics: The Science and Art of Transformation*, Hillsboro, Oregon, USA, Beyond Words Publishing.

14. Apigian, Aimie (2017), *Stuck Survival Responses in Attachment Trauma,* Trauma Healing Accelerated, May 18, 2017, draimie.com/stuck-survival-responses-in-attachment-trauma/. Accessed 11 June 2021

15. Newton, Consuella C.(2001), *The Inner Quest,* Kearney, NE, USA: Morris Publishing,

16. Vasudev, Jaggi, Sadhguru (2016), *Inner Engineering: A Yogi's Guide to Joy*, New York, New York, USA: Spiegel & Grau.

17. McTaggart, Lynne (2002), *The Field: The Quest for the Secret Force of the Universe*, New York, New York, USA: HarperCollins Publishers, Inc.

18. McTaggart, Lynne (2008), *The Intention Experiment: Using Your Thoughts to Change Your Life and the World*, New York, New York, USA: Simon & Schuster, Inc.

19. Chopra, Deepak (1994), *The Seven Spiritual Laws of Success: A Practical Guide to the Fulfillment of Your Dreams*, Novato, California, USA: New World Library.

20. Schimmel, Annemarie (1993), T*he Triumphal Sun: A Study of the Works of Jalaloddin Rumi*, Albany, New York, USA: State University of New York Press.

21. Mails, Thomas (1997), *The Hopi Survival Kit*, New York, New York, USA: ARKANA, Penguin Group.

22. Gregg, Susan (2000), *The Toltec Way*, Los Angeles, California, USA: Renaissance Books.

Definitions

Akasha (Akashic Field, Akashic Records, Universal Mind) – The Akasha is a field of information that holds the memory of all that has occurred, will occur or occurs across all.

Beingness – Beingness is the flow of creative principles, manifesting as an awareness of self beyond identity. Our essence is an expression of the creative principle of memory and our choice in each moment.

Chakra – Chakras are energy points in your body that correspond to bundles of nerves, major organs, and areas of our energetic body that affect our emotional and physical well-being[14].

Created pattern - A created pattern is a conceptual identification statement that underlies a behavior done repeatedly. For example, a created pattern may be the ritual of drinking coffee first thing in the morning. The created pattern identifies as 'I must have my coffee first thing in the morning.' A created pattern may be feeling betrayed by 'friends' repeatedly. The created pattern would then identify as 'My friends betray me.' This created pattern tells a story of hurt and harm repeatedly to solidify being a victim. The ritual of drinking a cup of coffee in the morning may not be limiting. However, the feeling and the created pattern of being betrayed by friends may have locked a person into a victim identity cycle. This created pattern may be limiting.

The foundation of all limiting patterns is fear. When there is an experience or a repeated experience of an instinctual response to a physical threat, and that response is not allowed to complete its process, that response will get stuck. We then develop limiting created patterns that we believe keep us safe. We adapt our lives and responses to those patterns and create emotional states, multiple created patterns, to stay safe. The origin of those stuck responses is not always from your life experiences. Intense reactions to trauma may have made physical changes in the genetics that may be inherited (epigenetics).

Emotional Release Therapy – Emotional Release Therapy is an energy healing method that involves an applied method of releasing stuck emotions that limit and create dysfunction.

Epigenetics – Epigenetics is the study of inherited changes that are not changes to the genes. Instead, the inherited change is reflected in how the gene is expressed. The change in expression is due to a chemical that is attached to the DNA. This chemical change is inherited.

Field – A field is a subtly defined space of influence. If I say, 'I am witness to the field of intention,' I have made an intention with an area of influence. A relationship between two people would also be a field. The relationship occupies space and contains energy which creates an area of influence, a field.

Harmony – In a state of harmony, you experience the flow of the creative principle; you experience grace. When you flow with the river of life, the creative principle, you experience the knowing of our nature. Our very essence is an expression of the creative principles of memory and our choice made in each moment.

Trigger – A trigger is a connection or link to trauma from your current life or ancestry that provokes an emotional response. A trigger can be a physical item, a sound, a smell, an image, a color, a person's voice, etcetera. For example, you are standing in line at a store, the woman in front of you is wearing perfume that reminds you of an aunt you loved. You are immediately overwhelmed with grief. That aunt passed away many years ago, and at that moment, you are overcome by sadness. The smell of the perfume was a trigger for your stuck grief.

Relationship – A relationship is a continuum of experience in space and time. A relationship is not a static feedback loop. Instead, a relationship is a flow of energy between connecting entities that continually creates your reality.

Contacting Valeria

If you have any questions about Remen $\bar{Q}$ or <u>Emotional Patterns,</u> send an email to rq@valeriamoore.com.

To sign up for my mail list, go to remen-q.com. I will notify you of upcoming workshops, new articles, and new books available.

Remen $\bar{Q}$ allows you to change your

reality across your infinite

multidimensional nature

Made in the USA
Monee, IL
24 September 2021